10-7-59

# Soviet Influence
# in Latin America:
# the Role of
# Economic Relations

# Soviet Influence
# in Latin America:
# the Role of
# Economic Relations

by
**ROBERT LORING ALLEN**

Published in Cooperation With the
Woodrow Wilson Department of Foreign Affairs,
University of Virginia

**Public Affairs Press, Washington D. C.**

# FOREWORD

Interest in Latin American economic affairs quickened in 1958 and 1959 as the economic position of the area grew so serious that even the most unperceptive observers could no longer fail to recognize Latin America's plight. North American political leadership has also received vivid demonstrations of the unrest that usually accompany deteriorating economic conditions in the area. An acceleration of contributions to the literature on the subject has already begun. Out of the universities, research organizations, international bodies, Congressional committees, and government agencies will come many useful studies. These efforts reflect a deep-seated conviction on the part of many scholars that Latin America, a crucial part of the free world, has fundamental economic problems not susceptible to tricky or easy solutions. Meaningful solutions will be found only in realistic but bold and imaginative thinking and actions by Latin Americans and their friends.

To compress the major considerations concerning the economic relations between two of the most important world regions—Latin America and the Soviet-East European bloc—into a few pages may be vain and quixotic and is certainly bound to be frustrating, due not only to the complexity of the topic, but also because of the swift-moving pace of events. An examination of the problem is justified, however, by the importance of the subject, by the chaotic state of the literature on the subject, and by the lessons in international commercial policy to be learned from this example.

In order to keep the study within manageable proportions, the author has deliberately avoided all but the most cursory treatment of trade before the Second World War and, indeed, in the postwar period particular emphasis is directed primarily at the years from 1952 through 1958. Nor is every last transaction or the latest protocol to each trade agreement examined in detail. The author has also shunned treatment of purely political questions, except those bearing directly on the economic relations.

This study, then, attempts a summary of the economic relations between Latin America and the Soviet Union and Eastern Europe, accompanied by an examination of the present posture and motives of the trading partners. The author has tried to describe and analyze the existing state of affairs without prescribing any course of action, either for the participants or for their other trading partners.

Any study of Soviet and East European foreign economic relations is confronted with various hazards, including heated emotions and controversies. In a period when the atmosphere of the "cold war" prevails, ideological inferences and partisan conclusions are almost inevitably drawn, even from statistical data, so that the presentation of facts in themselves becomes a challenging exercise. Preconceptions and stereotypes have in some instances led to undue emphasis upon one or another facet of Soviet and East European tactics in the vast literature which has developed on this subject in recent years.

Although the author's personal sympathies are generally opposed to Soviet economic and political concepts and practices, a studious attempt has been made to avoid highly interpretive judgments and to concentrate upon the exposition of the facts and upon closely reasoned and restrained analysis. An effort has been made to weigh the motives behind the actions of the parties directly concerned. The aim has been to record the salient features of Soviet and East European economic relations with Latin America in an objective, coherent fashion, with the evidence in full view, so that the reader may himself draw his own conclusions.

This work is the second in a series of monographic regional studies by the author designed to throw light on trade between Soviet Russia, Eastern Europe, and mainland China and their important trading partners. The first was *Middle Eastern Economic Relations with the Soviet Union, Eastern Europe and mainland China,* published in 1958 by the Woodrow Wilson Department of Foreign Affairs of the University of Virginia. The author, an associate professor of economics at the University of Virginia, is the director of a research project which, since 1956, has been systematically examining the commercial policy and relations of the Soviet bloc of countries.

The present study also comes in the wake of three important contributions to the literature on Soviet trade with underdeveloped countries: *Soviet Economic Aid* by Joseph Berliner, published by Frederick A. Praeger in 1958; *Financing Free World Trade with the Sino-Soviet Bloc* by Raymond Mikesell and Jack Behrman, published in 1958 by International Finance Section, Princeton University; and *Vneshniaia Torgovlia SSSR so stranami Asii, Afriki i Latinskoi Ameriki* edited by V. P. Gorunov, N. N. Inozemstsev, and V. B. Spandarian and published by Vneshtorgizdat in Moscow in 1958.

This work leans heavily on these general studies, as well as on the specialized data and discussions of Latin American trade appearing in *Direction of International Trade, International Financial Statistics, Vneshniaia Torgovlia SSSR za 1956 god, Vneshniaia Torgovlia SSSR za 1957 god,* the *Economic Survey (s) of Latin America,* the *Economic Bulletin (s) of Latin America,* other studies published by the Economic Commission for Latin America, United States Department of Commerce publications, United States Department of State publications, along with numerous monographs and articles on Latin America, and press dispatches.

The author gratefully acknowledges assistance from many people. To his colleagues in economics and foreign affairs at the University he feels a deep sense of gratitude for stimulation, interest, and the kind of atmosphere which makes research possible. Conversations with numerous specialists in departments of the United States government, international organizations, and private organizations were most useful.

The largest debt, however, is due to those people who worked with the author from day to day, particularly Mr. Craig Lovitt who did much of the statistical and tabular work, and also to Professor Stanley J. Zyzniewski, Dr. Som Prakash, Mr. V. D. Blinov, and Miss Susan Hunt, all of the University of Virginia, and to Professor C. F. Owen of William and Mary College who made a special study of Latin American oil requirements and problems. The author is grateful to his wife for her infinite patience, helpful criticisms, proofreading, and for her artistic talents on the charts.

ROBERT LORING ALLEN

*Charlottesville, Virginia*

# CONTENTS

## TABLES

## CHARTS

Latin America and the Soviet Union and Eastern Europe are both huge continental land areas whose combined foreign trade constitutes more than 15% of total world trade.[1] Both of the areas are rich in manpower and natural resources and both are still in the throes of economic development. Latin America, however, remains primarily dependent upon agricultural and mineral products. Both regions are growing rapidly economically, with Latin America lagging slightly and displaying somewhat more erratic progress, partly because of its more rapid rate of population growth, partly because its democratic states cannot and do not wish to take the stern measures necessary to depress consumption and increase investment, and partly because of Latin America's greater dependence on world markets.

The Soviet Union and Eastern Europe have recently begun to forsake their postwar trade isolation, creating a situation evidenced by a gradually expanding volume of trade not only with traditional trading partners, but also with primary producing countries, and by the alteration of the product-mix of their trade. The Soviet Union and Eastern Europe have begun to increase their capital goods export capabilities and have also imported in recent years greater quantities of primary products. Latin America has also expanded its trade in recent years, albeit more modestly, but continues to be plagued by surpluses of primary products, which constitute the main export commodity group.

Trade between the two areas has always been modest, as can be seen in Chart 1. In the prewar period Latin American exports to and imports from the Soviet Union and Eastern Europe were only slightly more than 1% of its total exports and imports as well as an equally small proportion of Soviet and East European trade. Until 1954, trade accounted for even a smaller proportion. Only since 1954 has the trade been sufficiently large to merit more than mere statistical attention.

Despite the still small volume of trade, the economic relations of Latin America with the Soviet Union and Eastern Europe have been the subject of a great deal of attention since 1954. Much of this discussion has been in the popular press and has tended to emphasize the

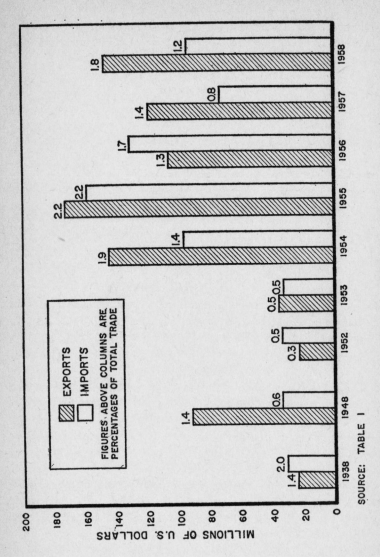

SOURCE: TABLE I

CHART 1 LATIN AMERICAN TRADE WITH THE SOVIET UNION
AND EASTERN EUROPE

2

importance and significance of the "new" trade between the two areas. Small events, such as a traveling trade delegation, or single transactions, such as the barter of a small amount of Soviet oil for Brazilian cacao, have received widespread comment, not only as a part of a major trend in world trade, but also as evidence of growing Soviet economic strength and capabilities as a trading nation.

Latin America has been lumped together with the Middle East, Asia, and Africa, as a battleground in economic competition and warfare between the "capitalist" countries under the leadership of the United States and the "socialist camp" under Soviet leadership. In their economic offensive, launched shortly after the death of Stalin, the Soviet Union and Eastern Europe have greatly expanded trade and extended credit to primary producing countries. Soviet motives have been regarded primarily as political, but the growth and changes in the Soviet economy in the past 30 years have also been taken as an added motive. As a result, it is frequently reported that the prestige and influence of the Soviet Union and Eastern Europe are increasing in the underdeveloped countries of the world, while the standing of the United States and other Western countries is declining, largely because of the Soviet "trade and aid" program.

Although this contention may be descriptive of other areas, such as Asia and the Middle East, its application to Latin America is far from complete. In the case of Latin America, the surprising element is not the expansion of trade, but rather that the expansion has been so modest. While the Soviet Union and Eastern Europe have gained a new respect in some countries of Latin America, this altered outlook has not been translated into concrete political or economic actions or influence favorable to the former. Latin America has not thus far broken ranks on any significant issue with Western Hemisphere solidarity. Unlike some other areas, Latin America has displayed no conscious inclination to permit trade with the Soviet Union and Eastern Europe to dictate or directly influence the decisions affecting its security or welfare.

A number of factors assist in explaining Latin America's unique relations with the Soviet Union and Eastern Europe. Three of the most important are: (1) a fundamental ideological and political antagonism between the thinking of the people as well as of the economic and political leadership of the two areas, (2) the inability of the Soviet Union and Eastern Europe to implement satisfactory commercial policies in their relations with Latin American countries, resulting in adverse terms of trade and unfavorable expectations in Latin America, and (3) the absence of a significant economic basis for large-scale trade between the two areas in terms of complementary export and import capabilities and requirements.

Sufficient data and experience are now at hand to undertake a careful examination of the economic relations between Latin America and the Soviet Union and Eastern Europe and to attempt to place these relations in proper perspective. It is the purpose of this paper to study the volume, composition, and direction of trade between the areas, to examine the commercial policies of both sides in the transactions, particularly the methods by which trade is conducted, and to explore the experiences of both the Soviet Union and Eastern Europe and Latin American countries in this trade, directing special attention to the problem of the terms of trade.

It is not enough, however, to have the facts straight. Almost as important as the trade itself are the conditions which give rise to it, the economic and trading position of Latin America and of the Soviet Union and Eastern Europe. While in most trade it may be safely assumed that commercial considerations are predominant, it is necessary to study closely the motives for trade between these two areas because of their unique characteristics. Only after an understanding of the objectives and of the economic posture of both areas has been gained is it possible to examine the key to the future magnitude, stability, and significance of this trade—the degree of competition and complementarity between the countries of Latin America and the Soviet Union and Eastern Europe.

It is hardly necessary to justify the study of trade between these two important world regions. Despite the small volume of trade, the adverse circumstances under which it is conducted, and its relatively modest potential, the trade itself, however small, is a significant avenue of influence. Trade relations also justify the presence of nationals from the Soviet Union and Eastern Europe in Latin America. Even presuming the most decorous behavior on their part, these nationals are provided with an opportunity to attempt to influence the local population and cooperate with like-minded citizens of the country. As in other areas, friendship societies are beginning to blossom in some Latin American countries, providing yet another method for ideological penetration. There could be no objection to wholesome ideological competition. The dangers lie in situations in which the Latin American people, for lack of information, misinformation, or a distortion of the facts, are unable to judge the merits of the case.

It must also be recognized that large-scale trading relations must start out from small trade. It is not inconceivable that should the Soviet Union so decide, trade could reach large proportions, even in the absence of a sound economic basis for the trade. In discussing the trade of the Soviet Union and Eastern Europe it is necessary to keep in mind the distinction between "economic" trade and "political" trade. The latter, a frequent characteristic of a missionary world movement operating under complete state control, is always possible, even if the likelihood seems small. For example, the Soviet Union, Eastern Europe, and mainland China in 1958 absorbed nearly one-third of the exports of the Middle East, even though it is clear that much of the trade is based upon arms deliveries by the Soviet Union and Czechoslovakia and the high priority the Soviet Union places upon the area from a political point of view.

Perhaps most important of all, however, is that an examination of economic relations between Latin America and the Soviet Union and Eastern Europe is a useful case study in commercial policy and operations. In this instance it can be determined how state trading countries undertake trade with primary producing countries, how the commercial policies of one group of nations adjust to those of another group of nations, what problems arise in the conduct of trade, and how they are resolved, and the impact of state trading practices on their trading partners.

The purpose of this section is to set the stage for a consideration of Latin American trade with the Soviet Union and Eastern Europe. The facts which are necessary for an understanding of this trade are contained in a series of statistical tables in this section. The analysis of these data and their implications are reserved for later sections.[1]

The principal characteristics of Soviet and East European trade with Latin American countries are: (1) low volume, (2) erratic and relatively large year-to-year changes in volume and the consequent absence of a trend, (3) a tendency toward a Latin American export surplus, (4) concentration of most trade among a few trading partners, and (5) instability in commodity composition.

*Volume.* Total Latin American trade turnover with the Soviet Union and Eastern Europe has never exceeded $350 million in any year and the average over the past seven years has been slightly less than $200 million. The export high was less than $175 million and exports have averaged about $107 million per year, while imports were greatest in value at less than $160 million and have averaged about $88 million per year during the last seven years. The highest levels for both exports and imports represent only slightly more than 2% of total Latin American exports and imports, but the average has been about 1%.

In 1958 trade turnover was less than $250 million, which was greater than in 1957, slightly higher than in 1956, but below trade in 1955, and about the same as trade in 1954. With 1955 as the base of 100, Latin American exports to the Soviet-East European area were 61 in 1956, 69 in 1957, and 85 in 1958. In 1952, the index stood at only 13. On the import side, with the same base, imports were 83 in 1956, 44 in 1957, and 60 in 1958. In 1952 imports were 22% of the 1955 level.

There is no apparent trend in exports, imports, or total trade. There was a build-up of trade between 1952 and 1955 (1953 imports were an exception), then a drop in 1956, and increases again since 1956 (except imports in 1957 and 1958—both below the 1956 level). During the past seven years, Latin America has had an export surplus

6

each year, save in 1952 and 1956. The total net export surplus with the Soviet Union and Eastern Europe for the last seven years was about the same as Latin American imports from that area in 1955, the peak year.

*Principal Trading Partners.* The principal Latin American trading partners in the Soviet bloc are the Soviet Union, Czechoslovakia, and Poland, as is indicated in Table 1. These three countries have shipped between 73% and 92% of all Soviet and East European exports to Latin America, an average of 87% during the past seven years. Of total Latin American exports to the Soviet and East European area, between 70% and 89% have been sold to these three countries, an average of 85% for the period.

The Soviet Union, Czechoslovakia, and Poland led all countries in both imports and exports for each year, except that Hungarian imports exceeded those of Poland in 1952 and the Soviet Union in 1957. Hungary is generally the fourth ranking trading partner. Bulgarian, East German, and Rumanian trade has been quite small— never exceeding $5 million in any year and usually much less. The Soviet Union is the leading exporter from the area to Latin America, with Czechoslovakia second. On the import side, Czechoslovakia is first and Poland second. Because of the relatively greater Czech imports, Czechoslovakia leads the Soviet Union in total trade turnover with Latin America.

The Soviet Union has had an import surplus with Latin America each year except 1952, when trade was balanced at an extremely low level. The total imbalance is well over twice Soviet exports in 1955, the year of its greatest exports. Czechoslovakia exported more to Latin America than it imported each year and Poland had a slight net export surplus for the seven years. These two countries are the only ones in the whole area which have demonstrated their ability to meet, even in a minimal fashion, their export commitments. Latin American exports to the Soviet Union and Eastern Europe have exceeded imports in every year except 1952, and again in 1956 when Polish and Czech exports more than offset the Soviet deficit. A part of the reason for Latin America's export surplus is the fact that Cuba has been a substantial exporter of sugar to the Soviet Union since 1955, accounting for 15% to 35% of total Latin American exports.

Argentina, Brazil, and Uruguay, aside from Cuba, are the leading Latin American trading partners of the Soviet Union and Eastern

Table 1

Trade of Twenty Latin American Republics with the Soviet Union and Eastern Europe
(millions of U.S. dollars)

| EXPORTS | 1938 | 1948 | 1952 | 1953 | 1954 | 1955 | 1956 | 1957 | 1958 |
|---|---|---|---|---|---|---|---|---|---|
| Total exports | 1,748.8 | 6,493.0 | 7,017.0 | 7,566.1 | 7,772.5 | 7,771.4 | 8,342.6 | 8,466.7 | 8,039.9 |
| Total exports to Soviet Union and Eastern Europe | 24.2 | 92.0 | 22.5 | 35.9 | 144.6 | 173.3 | 106.3 | 119.4 | 146.7 |
| Soviet Union | 1.1 | 12.4 | 0.1 | 10.2 | 66.3 | 72.6 | 31.8 | 57.9 | 53.4 |
| Bulgaria | | | | | | | 0.4 | 0.1 | 1.1 |
| Czechoslovakia | 11.3 | 28.5 | 12.7 | 10.1 | 27.8 | 43.1 | 36.0 | 25.9 | 35.6 |
| East Germany | | | | | | | 1.8 | 1.6 | 3.6 |
| Hungary | 1.3 | 1.1 | 5.1 | 2.8 | 11.1 | 11.8 | 15.3 | 7.1 | 10.2 |
| Poland | 10.2 | 30.2 | 3.6 | 10.4 | 31.6 | 42.9 | 17.5 | 25.5 | 35.8 |
| Rumania | 0.3 | 19.8 | 1.0 | 2.4 | 7.8 | 2.9 | 3.5 | 1.3 | 7.0 |
| **IMPORTS** | | | | | | | | | |
| Total imports | 1,541.7 | 5,996.7 | 7,322.0 | 6,362.0 | 7,069.4 | 7,307.5 | 7,551.2 | 8,745.4 | 8,142.6 |
| Total imports from Soviet Union and Eastern Europe | 30.7 | 34.4 | 34.2 | 32.9 | 96.7 | 158.6 | 131.0 | 70.5 | 94.3 |
| Soviet Union | 0.5 | 0.8 | 0.1 | — | 29.8 | 39.2 | 30.0 | 5.0 | 13.6 |
| Bulgaria | | | | | | | | | 0.6 |
| Czechoslovakia | 15.9 | 23.4 | 16.3 | 17.0 | 31.8 | 54.3 | 54.7 | 37.1 | 36.8 |
| East Germany | | | | | | 0.2 | 2.6 | 3.2 | 4.0 |
| Hungary | 5.5 | 0.6 | 7.9 | 4.9 | 7.5 | 17.9 | 18.5 | 5.6 | 3.9 |
| Poland | 8.7 | 4.9 | 7.5 | 8.0 | 22.6 | 43.4 | 23.0 | 19.6 | 33.1 |
| Rumania | 0.1 | 4.7 | 2.4 | 3.0 | 5.0 | 3.6 | 2.2 | | 2.3 |

Source:  Data for 1938, 1948, 1952-1957 are from *Direction of International Trade*, Joint Publication of the Statistical Office of the United Nations, International Monetary Fund, and International Bank for [...] been prorated, to cover the entire year, from incomplete reports in "Value Series-Free World Exports and Imports," International Economic Analysis Division, Bureau of Foreign Commerce, United States Department of Commerce, January, 1959.

Europe. Between 1952 and 1958 these three countries provided between 63% and 98% of all exports to the Soviet Union and Eastern Europe. As mentioned, since 1955 Cuba has become an important exporter. These four countries, for all practical purposes, account for all of Latin American exports. Argentina is clearly in the lead, with Brazil second. Cuba has been third since 1955, except in 1957 when it exported more than either Argentina or Brazil.

Argentina, Brazil, and Uruguay are also the leading importers from

Table 2

Trade of the Soviet Union and Eastern Europe with Latin America

(millions of U.S. dollars)

| EXPORTS | 1938 | 1948 | 1952 | 1953 | 1954 | 1955 | 1956 | 1957 | 1958 |
|---|---|---|---|---|---|---|---|---|---|
| Total exports to Latin America | 30.7 | 34.4 | 34.2 | 32.9 | 96.7 | 158.6 | 131.0 | 70.5 | 94.3 |
| Argentina | 17.3 | 15.6 | 21.4 | 17.1 | 71.3 | 110.2 | 58.1 | 15.4 | 53.0 |
| Brazil | 5.1 | 11.8 | 5.8 | 9.7 | 18.8 | 38.2 | 46.2 | 38.2 | 23.6 |
| Chile | 0.3 | 0.3 | | | 0.1 | 1.3 | 2.3 | 0.7 | 0.1 |
| Colombia | 2.3 | 0.4 | 0.4 | 0.8 | 0.9 | 1.2 | 1.4 | 1.6 | 2.4 |
| Cuba | 0.7 | 0.4 | 0.9 | 0.7 | 0.8 | 1.3 | 2.6 | 2.5 | 3.0 |
| Ecuador | 0.1 | 0.2 | 0.3 | 0.2 | | | | | 0.1 |
| Haiti | 0.1 | | 0.3 | 0.3 | 0.6 | 1.2 | 2.0 | | |
| Mexico | 1.1 | 0.9 | 1.1 | 0.7 | 0.8 | 0.9 | 2.1 | 2.3 | 2.2 |
| Paraguay | 0.1 | | | | | | 2.0 | 0.1 | |
| Peru | 0.8 | 0.6 | 1.0 | 0.3 | | 0.2 | 0.6 | 1.4 | 1.2 |
| Uruguay | 1.9 | 1.3 | 0.9 | 0.3 | 1.3 | 2.5 | 10.5 | 4.9 | 4.4 |
| Venezuela | 0.1 | 2.1 | 1.2 | 1.5 | | | 1.8 | 2.3 | 4.3 |
| Others | 0.8 | 0.8 | 0.9 | 1.3 | 2.1 | 1.6 | 1.4 | 1.1 | -- |

| IMPORTS | 1938 | 1948 | 1952 | 1953 | 1954 | 1955 | 1956 | 1957 | 1958 |
|---|---|---|---|---|---|---|---|---|---|
| Total imports from Latin America | 24.2 | 92.0 | 22.5 | 35.9 | 144.6 | 173.3 | 106.3 | 119.4 | 146.7 |
| Argentina | 13.7 | 49.0 | 14.5 | 23.5 | 97.7 | 81.6 | 41.2 | 29.0 | 59.2 |
| Brazil | 4.2 | 20.1 | 6.4 | 10.3 | 21.5 | 42.1 | 39.4 | 38.8 | 33.5 |
| Chile | 0.5 | 7.2 | | 0.1 | 2.0 | 0.3 | | | |
| Colombia | 0.7 | | | | | 1.2 | 0.9 | | 0.1 |
| Cuba | 0.2 | 0.1 | 0.1 | 0.8 | 0.8 | 37.0 | 15.6 | 42.0 | 27.4 |
| Ecuador | 0.2 | | | 0.1 | | 0.1 | 0.2 | 1.4 | 0.2 |
| Haiti | | | | | | 0.1 | | | |
| Mexico | 1.0 | 11.8 | 0.4 | 0.2 | | 0.4 | 0.1 | 0.3 | 0.5 |
| Paraguay | | | | | | | | | |
| Peru | 0.1 | 1.3 | | | | | | | 1.2 |
| Uruguay | 3.3 | 2.5 | 1.1 | 0.9 | 22.6 | 10.5 | 7.8 | 7.8 | 24.6 |
| Venezuela | | | | | | | 1.0 | 0.1 | |
| Others | 0.3 | -- | -- | -- | -- | -- | 0.1 | | |

Source: As in Table 1. The data collected and collated for this study vary not only with Soviet data but also with statistics found in other available sources. For example, official Paraguayan statistics report exports of $1.2 million to Hungary and $0.6 million to Czechoslovakia in 1956, as well as small shipments to those countries in 1954 and 1955. These same reports, however, were evidently not made to the compilers of the Direction of International Trade and do not therefore appear in the data contained in the tables used in this study.

the Soviet Union and Eastern Europe, the three importing 83% to 95% of total imports during the past seven years. Again, Argentina leads by a wide margin. In total trade turnover, Argentina's share is somewhat less than 60% and Brazil's share about 30%. Of the remainder, Uruguay and Cuba account for the greatest proportion. Argentina was the leading importer in every year except 1957, when Brazil, usually in second place, imported more.

Over the seven-year period, Argentina's trade has been approximately balanced. Brazil's trade has also been about the same both ways. Uruguay's exports have been three times its imports and that country has had an export surplus with the Soviet Union and Eastern Europe every year except in 1955. The sizeable Cuban export surplus derives from its negligible imports from the Soviet Union and Eastern Europe.

*Indirect Trade.* The direct trade between Latin American countries and the Soviet Union and Eastern Europe does not account for all trade on the Latin American export side. Brazil and Uruguay in particular have sold goods to the Netherlands and other West European countries for re-export to the Soviet Union or some East European country. Such trade is recorded in Latin American statistics for the country which is officially designated as the recipient, not the ultimate buyer. As an example, the Brazilian finance minister announced in March, 1958, that he had authorized the sale of 100,000 bags of coffee to the Soviet Union through a British company in exchange for either cash or goods. Uruguay shipped at least $6 million in wool to China in 1956 through the Netherlands.

Indirect trade takes place when official trade relations do not exist (as was the case between Brazil and the Soviet Union until recently), when a trade agreement is not in effect, or when it is profitable to the Latin American exporter to circumvent the terms of the trade agreement or avoid the operations of the clearing system. The amount of this indirect trade is, however, not large and varies considerably from year to year.

*Data Reliability.* Lest one develop too much confidence in the straightforward and unequivocal appearance of the statistics of trade, it may be useful to inject a sobering thought. It is seldom that trading partners agree on the amount of trade which takes place

Table 3

Soviet Trade with Latin America

(millions of U.S. dollars)

| | 1954 | | 1955 | | 1956 | | 1957 | |
|---|---|---|---|---|---|---|---|---|
| **Argentina** | | | | | | | | |
| Exports | 35.9 | (29.8) | 24.0 | (39.1) | 19.1 | (26.7) | 4.7 | ( 4.6) |
| Imports | 41.0 | (45.6) | 28.2 | (29.7) | 13.0 | (16.7) | 20.8 | (14.1) |
| Balance | -5.1 | (-15.8) | -4.2 | (+9.4) | +6.1 | (+10.0) | -16.1 | (-9.5) |
| **Brazil** | | | | | | | | |
| Exports | | | -- | -- | -- | | | |
| Imports | | | 1.9 | ( 0.7) | 3.1 | | | |
| Balance | | | -1.9 | (-0.7) | -3.1 | | | |
| **Uruguay** | | | | | | | | |
| Exports | -- | -- | 0.3 | ( 0.1) | 2.9 | ( 3.2) | 0.1 | ( 0.3) |
| Imports | 29.1 | (19.9) | 10.0 | ( 4.6) | 12.3 | ( 0.4) | 18.1 | ( 1.8) |
| Balance | -29.1 | (-19.9) | -9.7 | (-4.5) | -9.4 | (+2.8) | -18.0 | (-1.5) |
| **Total** | | | | | | | | |
| Exports | 35.9 | (29.8) | 24.3 | (39.2) | 22.0 | (29.9) | 4.8 | ( 4.9) |
| Imports | 70.1 | (65.5) | 40.1 | (35.0) | 28.4 | (17.1) | 38.9 | (15.9) |
| Balance | -34.2 | (-35.7) | -15.8 | (+4.2) | -6.4 | (+12.8) | -34.1 | (-11.0) |

Source: Vneshniaia Torgovlia SSSR za 1956 god, Moscow, 1958, Vneshniaia Torgovlia
SSSR za 1957 god, Moscow, 1957, and Vneshniaia Torgovlia SSSR so stravanii
Asii, Afriki, i Latinskoi Ameriki, Moscow, 1958. Data in parentheses are
from Direction of International Trade, Vol. IX, No. 10, 1958.

between them. Table 3 shows the trade of three Latin American
countries with the Soviet Union as reported both by the Latin
American countries and by the Soviet Union. It is worth noting that
in none of the 16 examples are the data identical. In only five cases
are the data from the two different sources within 20% of one another.
In five instances one figure is at least double the figure reported by
the trading partner. Many divergencies can be accounted for by
the differences in f.o.b. and c.i.f. prices, still others by reporting
systems, method of valuation, time lags, and re-exports. Most of the
differences can be explained, but Soviet data tend to contain dis-
crepancies which are intractable.[2]

Table 4

Argentina's Trade with the Soviet Union and Eastern Europe

(millions of U.S. dollars)

| EXPORTS | 1938 | 1948 | 1952 | 1953 | 1954 | 1955 | 1956 | 1957 | 1958 |
|---|---|---|---|---|---|---|---|---|---|
| Total exports | 461.0 | 1,626.7 | 709.4 | 1,165.7 | 1,079.9 | 928.6 | 943.8 | 974.8 | 964.4 |
| Total exports to Soviet Union and Eastern Europe | 13.7 | 49.0 | 14.5 | 23.5 | 97.7 | 81.6 | 41.2 | 29.0 | 59.2 |
| Soviet Union | 1.1 | 1.7 | -- | 9.3 | 45.6 | 29.7 | 16.7 | 14.1 | 9.8 |
| Bulgaria | | | | | | | | | 0.6 |
| Czechoslovakia | 5.9 | 19.0 | 6.1 | 0.5 | 13.3 | 17.8 | 11.0 | 5.7 | 16.2 |
| East Germany | | | | | | | | | 0.8 |
| Hungary | 0.8 | 1.0 | 5.0 | 2.8 | 8.5 | 3.5 | 4.5 | 1.5 | 7.2 |
| Poland | 5.7 | 9.2 | 2.4 | 8.5 | 23.5 | 27.7 | 6.0 | 7.7 | 18.0 |
| Rumania | 0.2 | 18.1 | 1.0 | 2.4 | 6.8 | 2.9 | 3.0 | -- | 6.6 |
| **IMPORTS** | | | | | | | | | |
| Total imports | 490.8 | 1,590.4 | 1,195.8 | 876.8 | 954.8 | 1,172.6 | 1,127.6 | 1,310.4 | 1,220.0 |
| Total imports from Soviet Union and Eastern Europe | 17.3 | 15.6 | 21.4 | 17.1 | 71.3 | 110.2 | 58.1 | 15.4 | 53.0 |
| Soviet Union | 0.5 | 0.6 | | | 29.8 | 39.1 | 26.7 | 4.6 | 10.4 |
| Bulgaria | | | | | | | | | 0.5 |
| Czechoslovakia | 6.9 | 8.2 | 4.4 | 3.8 | 12.2 | 25.1 | 16.1 | 6.0 | 15.2 |
| East Germany | | | | | | | | | 0.3 |
| Hungary | 3.7 | 0.3 | 7.6 | 4.5 | 6.2 | 9.9 | 6.4 | 1.5 | 1.7 |
| Poland | 6.1 | 1.8 | 7.0 | 5.8 | 18.1 | 32.5 | 6.7 | 3.3 | 23.4 |
| Rumania | 0.1 | 4.7 | 2.4 | 3.0 | 5.0 | 3.6 | 2.2 | | 1.5 |

Source:  As in Table 1.

*Argentina.* The Soviet Union is the principal purchaser from Argentina in the Soviet-East European area, with Poland second and Czechoslovakia third (Table 4). Bulgaria and East Germany buy practically nothing. The three most important buyers are also the three most important sellers to Argentina. The Soviet Union, however, has been in a deficit position, while both Czechoslovakia and Poland have been in a slight surplus position with Argentina. The proportion of Argentinian exports to the Soviet Union and Eastern Europe to total exports has been quite small. The year of largest exports, 1954, was also the year of the highest proportion, 9%, about one-half of which was purchased by the Soviet Union. In 1955, Argentina purchased 9% of its imports from the Soviet-East European area, of which the Soviet Union provided slightly more than one-third.

*Brazil.* The unique characteristic of Brazilian trade is the absence of trade with the Soviet Union (Table 5). There has been some indirect trade, particularly through the Netherlands, but only negligible amounts of direct trade. The level of trade with Eastern Europe is considerably below that of Argentina, both on the export and import side. The principal buyers and sellers from Brazil are Czechoslovakia, Hungary, and Poland. Trade with all three has been approximately balanced over the last seven years. As a proportion of total Brazilian exports Eastern Europe bought 3% in 1955 (more than one-half bought by Czechoslovakia) and sold to Brazil 4% of its imports in 1956 (again Czechoslovakia provided about one-half).

*Uruguay.* Uruguayan trade with the Soviet Union and Eastern Europe is quite small, although exports reached a high level in 1958, accounting for nearly 16% (Table 6). The Soviet Union bought more than three-fifths of that amount. For the most part, the Soviet Union has led as the principal importer of Uruguayan goods, although Czechoslovakia, Poland, and in the last three years East Germany have also been important purchasers. Czechoslovakia and the Soviet Union have also been the principal exporters to Uruguay, the largest proportion for the entire Soviet-East European area having been about 5% in 1956.

*Commodity Composition.* The commodity composition of Soviet and East European trade with Latin American countries is illustrated

Table 5

Brazil's Trade with the Soviet Union and Eastern Europe
(millions of U.S. dollars)

| | 1938 | 1948 | 1952 | 1953 | 1954 | 1955 | 1956 | 1957 | 1958 |
|---|---|---|---|---|---|---|---|---|---|
| **EXPORTS** | | | | | | | | | |
| Total exports | 289.2 | 1,172.7 | 1,408.8 | 1,539.3 | 1,561.8 | 1,423.3 | 1,482.6 | 1,391.3 | 2,155.1 |
| Total exports to Soviet Union and Eastern Europe | 4.2 | 20.1 | 6.4 | 10.3 | 21.5 | 42.1 | 39.4 | 38.8 | 33.5 |
| Soviet Union | | | | | | 0.7 | | | 1.0 |
| Bulgaria | | | | | | | | | |
| Czechoslovakia | 1.7 | 2.3 | 5.4 | 8.7 | 12.2 | 21.5 | 20.3 | 17.0 | 14.2 |
| East Germany | | | | | | | | | |
| Hungary | 0.1 | | | | 2.2 | | | | |
| Poland | 2.3 | 16.1 | 1.0 | 1.6 | 6.1 | 7.0 | 9.0 | 5.3 | 2.2 |
| Rumania | 0.1 | 1.7 | | | 1.0 | 12.9 | 10.1 | 16.5 | 16.1 |
| **IMPORTS** | | | | | | | | | |
| Total imports | 294.8 | 1,134.2 | 2,009.5 | 1,318.6 | 1,633.5 | 1,306.8 | 1,233.9 | 1,488.2 | 1,242.0 |
| Total imports from Soviet Union and Eastern Europe | 5.1 | 11.8 | 5.8 | 9.7 | 18.8 | 38.2 | 46.2 | 38.2 | 23.6 |
| Soviet Union | | | | | | | | | 1.0 |
| Bulgaria | | | | | | | | | |
| Czechoslovakia | 3.6 | 8.6 | 5.5 | 7.8 | 13.5 | 21.4 | 22.7 | 18.2 | 12.3 |
| East Germany | | | | | | | | | |
| Hungary | | | | | | | | 1.2 | |
| Poland | 0.4 | 0.1 | 0.3 | 1.9 | 1.0 | 6.5 | 8.9 | 4.1 | 1.4 |
| Rumania | 1.1 | 3.1 | | | 4.3 | 10.3 | 14.6 | 14.7 | 8.9 |

Source: As in Table 1.

Table 6

Uruguay's Trade with the Soviet Union and Eastern Europe
(millions of U.S. dollars)

| EXPORTS | 1938 | 1948 | 1952 | 1953 | 1954 | 1955 | 1956 | 1957 | 1958 |
|---|---|---|---|---|---|---|---|---|---|
| Total exports | 61.6 | 178.9 | 208.9 | 269.8 | 249.0 | 183.7 | 211.1 | 128.3 | 156.1 |
| Total exports to Soviet Union and Eastern Europe | 3.3 | 2.5 | 1.1 | 0.9 | 22.6 | 10.5 | 7.8 | 7.8 | 24.6 |
| Soviet Union | | | | | 19.9 | 4.6 | 0.4 | 1.8 | 15.2 |
| Bulgaria | | | | 0.2 | | | 0.1 | 0.1 | 0.5 |
| Czechoslovakia | 1.6 | 0.6 | 0.9 | 0.5 | 1.8 | 2.4 | 3.4 | 2.7 | 3.5 |
| East Germany | | | | | | | 1.8 | 1.6 | 2.7 |
| Hungary | 0.4 | | | | | | | | 0.8 |
| Poland | 1.3 | 1.9 | 0.2 | 0.2 | 0.9 | 1.2 | 0.8 | 0.3 | 1.5 |
| Rumania | | | | | | 2.3 | 1.3 | 1.3 | 0.4 |
| IMPORTS | | | | | | | | | |
| Total imports | 61.6 | 201.4 | 257.2 | 195.2 | 274.5 | 226.0 | 205.8 | 226.4 | 104.4 |
| Total imports from Soviet Union and Eastern Europe | 1.9 | 1.3 | 0.9 | 0.3 | 1.3 | 2.5 | 10.5 | 4.9 | 4.4 |
| Soviet Union | | | | | | 0.1 | 3.2 | 0.3 | 0.4 |
| Bulgaria | | | | | | | | | 0.1 |
| Czechoslovakia | 0.7 | 1.3 | 0.9 | 0.3 | 1.2 | 1.5 | 3.8 | 1.5 | 0.9 |
| East Germany | | | | | | 0.2 | 2.6 | 2.0 | 2.3 |
| Hungary | 0.9 | | | | | | 0.7 | | 0.3 |
| Poland | 0.3 | | | | 0.1 | 0.7 | 0.2 | | |
| Rumania | | | | | | | | 1.1 | 0.4 |

Source:   As in Table 1.

in Tables 7 and 8.  It is clear from a cursory examination of these
tables that commodity composition has shifted radically from year
to year.  In one year none of a given product will be imported by
a Latin American country from one of its trading partners and the
next year a substantial proportion of its imports of that product will
come from the same country.  In other instances a Latin American
country will export only one product in substantial proportion; the
next year, it will export only a very small percentage of that same
product.  It is also worth noting that most Latin American imports
have not been machinery and equipment.  Rather, most of the
imports have been raw materials—forestry products, fuels, crude
materials, chemicals, and partly fabricated items such as iron and
steel products.

Table 7

Commodity Composition of East European Trade with Argentina,

Brazil, and Uruguay

(percentages)

Argentina

| IMPORTS | 1953 | 1956 | 1957 |
|---|---|---|---|
| Machinery (including electric) | 29.7 | 21.8 | 35.0 |
| Transport and communication equipment | 17.3 | 38.1 | 16.5 |
| Coal, coke and briquettes | 21.5 | 3.0 | 28.2 |
| Forestry products (excluding paper) | 17.1 | 11.1 | 0.2 |
| Glass and pottery | 9.3 | 1.3 | |
| Chemicals (excluding fertilizers) | 0.9 | 1.7 | 4.5 |
| Building materials (manufactured) | 0.9 | 1.8 | 3.2 |
| Iron and steel | | 13.3 | 2.5 |
| Paper | | 2.8 | 5.3 |
| Crude minerals, cement and fertilizers | | 3.4 | |
| Dairy products (including honey) | 2.2 | | |

| EXPORTS | 1953 | 1956 | 1957 |
|---|---|---|---|
| Fur skins and hides | 62.4 | 59.6 | 39.4 |
| Wool | 19.2 | 4.0 | 32.8 |
| Chemicals (excluding fertilizers) | 15.6 | 10.0 | 13.2 |
| Meat and livestock | | 6.4 | 7.9 |
| Cereals | 2.5 | 16.3 | 2.4 |
| Oil-seeds, oils and fats | | 0.5 | 1.6 |
| Dairy products (including honey) | | 2.5 | |

Table 7 (continued)

## Commodity Composition of East European Trade with Argentina, Brazil, and Uruguay

### (percentages)

#### Brazil

| IMPORTS | 1953 | 1956 | 1957 |
|---|---|---|---|
| Machinery and equipment (including electric) | 27.6 | 21.6 | 17.8 |
| Crude minerals, cement and fertilizers | 27.4 | 17.6 | 6.8 |
| Iron and steel | | 15.8 | 33.2 |
| Cereals | 30.5 | 6.8 | 10.3 |
| Chemicals (excluding fertilizers) | 3.2 | 16.3 | 9.6 |
| Transport and communication equipment | 2.6 | 8.4 | 7.1 |
| Cotton and other textile fibers | | 2.3 | 3.4 |
| Miscellaneous foods and beverages | 2.1 | 1.4 | 4.8 |
| Coal, coke and briquettes | | 1.3 | 1.1 |
| Forestry products (excluding paper) | | 1.2 | 0.9 |
| Paper | 0.9 | 1.6 | 0.5 |
| Glass and pottery | 3.2 | 1.1 | 0.7 |
| Consumer durables | 0.6 | 0.8 | 0.5 |

| EXPORTS | 1953 | 1956 | 1957 |
|---|---|---|---|
| Coffee and other stimulants | 56.2 | 53.9 | 44.4 |
| Cotton and other textile fibers | 1.6 | 26.6 | 18.9 |
| Fur skins and hides | 22.3 | 11.3 | 7.6 |
| Iron and steel | 10.7 | 3.8 | 11.2 |
| Oil-seeds, oils and fats | | 2.7 | 14.5 |
| Sugar | 8.7 | | |
| Meat and livestock | | | 1.8 |
| Tobacco | | 0.5 | 1.1 |

#### Uruguay

| IMPORTS | |
|---|---|
| Cotton and other textile fibers | 23.1 |
| Iron and steel | 16.4 |
| Transport and communication equipment | 14.2 |
| Machinery and equipment (including electric) | 13.3 |
| Crude minerals, cement and fertilizers | 9.1 |
| Chemicals (excluding fertilizers) | 8.6 |
| Building materials (manufactured) | 4.0 |
| Paper | 2.2 |
| Glass and pottery | 1.3 |

| EXPORTS | | |
|---|---|---|
| Wool | 60.0 | 54.7 |
| Fur skins and hides | 19.8 | 29.6 |
| Meat and livestock | 12.4 | 13.9 |
| Oil-seeds, oils and fats | 3.8 | 1.1 |
| Cereals | 2.5 | |

Derived from data in "Country by Commodity Series," International Economic Analysis Division, Bureau of Foreign Commerce, United States Department of Commerce.

The statistical and factual picture which emerges concerning Latin American trade with the Soviet Union and Eastern Europe is that it represents, both on the export and import side, a low level and a small proportion of Latin American trade. While total trade is

## Table 8

### Commodity Composition of Soviet Trade with Argentina and Uruguay

#### (percentages)

#### Argentina

| IMPORTS | 1953 | 1956 | 1957 |
|---|---|---|---|
| Iron and steel | | 67.3 | 64.4 |
| Forestry products (excluding paper) | | 19.9 | 1.7 |
| Petroleum and petroleum products | | 5.9 | |
| Crude minerals, cement and fertilizers | | 3.4 | |
| Machinery (including electric) | | 1.5 | 13.1 |
| Paper | | | 1.1 |
| Chemicals (excluding fertilizers) | | 0.9 | 7.7 |
| Transport and communication equipment | | 0.7 | 9.6 |

| EXPORTS | | | |
|---|---|---|---|
| Meat and livestock | 21.7 | 14.2 | 8.3 |
| Dairy products (including honey) | 51.9 | | |
| Wool | . | 11.2 | 43.7 |
| Fur skins and hides | 10.4 | 74.4 | 43.7 |
| Oil-seeds, oils and fats | 16.0 | | |
| Chemicals (excluding fertilizers) | | | 4.1 |

#### Uruguay

| IMPORTS | | | |
|---|---|---|---|
| Iron and steel | | 28.5 | |
| Chemicals (excluding fertilizers) | | 42.3 | |
| Crude minerals, cement and fertilizers | | 9.4 | |
| Petroleum and petroleum products | | 6.2 | |
| Machinery and equipment (including electric) | | 4.0 | |
| Transport and communication equipment | | 5.2 | |
| Textiles and clothing | | 1.7 | |
| Consumer durables | | 1.1 | |

| EXPORTS | | | |
|---|---|---|---|
| Wool | | 100.0 | 5.8 |
| Meat and livestock | | | 73.6 |
| Fur skins and hides | | | 20.6 |

Source: Derived from data in "Country by Commodity Series," International Economic Analysis Division, Bureau of Foreign Commerce, United States Department of Commerce.

approximately balanced there is a consistent tendency for Latin America to show an export surplus. Three countries—the Soviet Union, Czechoslovakia, and Poland, in that order—are the principal Soviet-East European trading partners. Another three countries—Argentina, Brazil, and Uruguay, in that order—are the principal Latin American trading partners, with Cuba recently emerging as an exporter to the Soviet Union. While trade in recent years has been substantially larger than in the earlier period, it has demonstrated radical annual fluctuations over the past five years. The commodity composition, which is basically a raw materials for raw materials exchange, has also shifted noticeably from year to year.

The outstanding characteristic of trade and commercial policy in the economic relations of Latin America with the Soviet-East European area is the high degree to which this trade is regulated, controlled, or conducted by the governments involved. On the Soviet-East European side this situation is, of course, to be expected, since all of these countries have a complete state monopoly and monopsony of their foreign trade.

Despite a trend in overall Latin American trade toward liberalization of trade and multilateral payments, it has been necessary for Latin America to impose much greater governmental supervision on that small proportion of its trade with the Soviet Union and Eastern Europe than its trade with other areas. This has been made mandatory because of the insistence of the Soviet Union and Eastern Europe and in order to cope effectively with their state trading organizations and to maintain Latin American bargaining strength.[1] In general, however, Latin America, because of its weaker bargaining position, has adjusted its policies to fit those of its trading partners except when, in order to protect its interests, it has been necessary for Latin America to insist upon certain positive measures of assurance.

*Bilateral Aspects.* The essential ingredient of trade policy is one-to-one bilateralism conducted under highly specific bilateral trade and payments agreements. Under these agreements the quantities and prices of products exchanged are negotiated. In order to understand Latin American trade with the Soviet Union and Eastern Europe it is necessary to examine in some detail the provisions of these agreements, as listed in Tables 9 and 10.

Another significant element in Soviet-East European commercial policy is a large-scale trade promotion program. Delegations from the Soviet Union and Eastern Europe frequently visit in Latin America and Latin American government officials and business leaders are invited to the Soviet Union and East European countries to foster trade. Some of these countries maintain permanent trade delegations in Latin America and exhibits of Soviet industrial products are no longer a rarity. Along with trade promotion at the goods exchange level, spokesmen for the Soviet Union and Eastern

Europe have offered credit and technical assistance to Latin American countries and have extolled the potential benefits of larger scale trading.[2]

For the most part trade and payments agreements are negotiated between officials representing their respective governments, thus committing the governments to specified performance under the pact. For the Soviet Union and Eastern Europe this is perfectly normal because only the government is empowered to make foreign trade decisions. In Latin America, however, foreign trade is principally in the hands of private individuals and organizations and even the government of a country cannot assure the trading partners that private exporters will sell or importers buy enough to meet the targets in the agreements or that trade will be balanced. Argentina prior to 1955 experimented with a state trading organization, but abandoned it with a change in political regime. The governments of Latin America can and do make sufficient import licenses available and encourage importers to import from the Soviet Union and Eastern Europe. The governments also use their good offices to acquaint exporters with Soviet and East European trading organizations, thus lending respectability to their operations. Perhaps equally important, the government on its own account or acting as the agent for private interests, may conduct some of the trade itself.

*Non-Agreement Trade.* Trade is carried on by three other devices, even in the absence of a formal trade agreement. In some cases, most notably Cuba, the Latin American country simply contracts to sell a product to the Soviet Union or an East European country for cash, either dollars or sterling. In other instances, a specific barter agreement is arranged. This is a one-time, single-transaction agreement in which a Latin American country agrees to buy a particular amount of goods in exchange for a specified amount of its exports. There is no formal payments mechanism, although the transaction may be handled through an established clearing account if the countries concerned also have a payments agreement. In some cases the barter agreements run for a period of time and permit exchanges in addition to the initial trade, and thus begin to partake of the characteristics of trade agreements. As mentioned earlier, a small amount of trade between Latin American countries and the Soviet Union and Eastern Europe is performed through third countries, such as Great Britain or the Netherlands. Legally, this indirect trade is not trade;

Brazil lists its exports to the Netherlands, for example, although it may be known that the ultimate destination is the Soviet Union.

These other methods for conducting trade may exist alongside trade through a regular trade agreement but in most cases they are unique and are designed to handle trade when an agreement is lacking. The absence of diplomatic recognition or relations is the most frequent cause for employing devices other than the formal trade agreement. There is an evident readiness to depart from its standard trading procedures underlying the eagerness of the Soviet-East European area to establish a trading "beachhead" in Latin America. For the same reason, not all trade and barter agreements or contracts are between governments. On the Latin American side, a bank or a trade association may be the signatory, rather than the government.

*Trade Agreements.* In the last three year there have been 25 formal trade agreements in effect between six Latin American countries and the Soviet Union and the six East European countries. Argentina and Uruguay have agreements with each country; Brazil has agreements with all countries except the Soviet Union and Bulgaria; Colombia had agreements with Czechoslovakia and East Germany; Mexico had an agreement with Czechoslovakia; and Paraguay had agreements with Czechoslovakia, Hungary, and Poland. There is no evidence to indicate that any of the Colombian, Mexican, or Paraguayan agreements were in force in 1958. Chile, Colombia, and Cuba have exported to the Soviet Union under formal contracts; Chile has bartered goods with Czechoslovakia, East Germany, and Hungary. Colombia has also had barter agreements with Hungary. In the last three years more than 90% of Latin American imports from the Soviet Union and Eastern Europe have been under these agreements and nearly all of Latin American exports have been covered by agreements. The trade agreements in force in 1958 are listed in Table 9.

Unlike Soviet and East European agreements with many other countries, which are for three years, sometimes even longer, Latin American agreements are for one year. Barter agreements and contracts, of course, terminate at the end of the transaction. The trade agreements nearly all provide for annual renewal without specific negotiations but also permit unilateral renunciation on 90 days' notice. The trade agreements usually provide a relatively simple listing of products or product categories to be exchanged. In

Table 9

Trade Agreements in Force in 1958 between Latin American
Countries and the Soviet Union and Eastern Europe*

| | Soviet Union | Bulgaria | Czechoslovakia | East Germany | Hungary | Poland | Rumania |
|---|---|---|---|---|---|---|---|
| Argentina | T,R,L, Q,E,X | T,R,L,E | T,R,L,Q E,X | T,E,I | T,R,L, Q,E,X | T,R,L, Q,E,X | T,R,L, X |
| Brazil | B | | B,T,R,L, Q,X | T,R,L | T,R,L, E | B,T,R, L,Q,E, X | T,L |
| Chile | C | | B,P,N | B,P,L, E,N | B,P,E | | |
| Colombia | B | | B,T,L, NQ,N | T,L,Q, E,N | B,N | | |
| Mexico | | | T,R,L, NQ | | | | |
| Paraguay | | | T,P,R,L, NQ,I | | T,P,R, L,NQ,I | T,P,L, I | |
| Uruguay | T,R,L, NQ,E,I | T,I | T,R,L,E | T,R,L, E,I | T,R,L, Q,I | T,R,I | T,R,L, I |

Key:

| | | | |
|---|---|---|---|
| T | - Trade agreement | Q | - Quotas |
| B | - Barter | NQ | - No quotas |
| C | - Contract | E | - Balanced trade |
| P | - Previous agreement - not in force in 1958 | X | - Re-exports prohibited |
| R | - Annual tacit renewal | N | - Non-governmental |
| L | - Commodity lists | I | - Interbank agreement |

* No known agreements in 1958 for Bolivia, Costa Rica, Dominican Republic, Ecuador, El Salvador, Guatemala, Haiti, Honduras, Nicaragua, Panama, Peru, and Venezuela. Cuba sells to the Soviet Union on a contract basis only.

Source: Trade Agreements and Other Trade Accords with Soviet Bloc Countries, U.S. Department of State, Washington, 1955-58; International Trade News Bulletin, General Agreement on Tariffs and Trade, Geneva, 1951-1959; Exchange Restrictions, First to Ninth Annual Reports, International Monetary Fund, Washington, 1950-1958; data furnished by U.S. Department of Commerce, Washington; Raymond Mikesell and Jack Behrman, Financing Free World Trade with the Sino-Soviet Bloc, International Finance Section, Princeton, 1958, Appendix 1; and numerous press dispatches.

the past quotas were specified on occasion, but this practice has now been abandoned. The individual transactions under the trade agreements are carried out by ordinary commercial contracts. Most of the agreements specify an equal value of trade for both countries. In a few cases the trade is deliberately unbalanced in order to pay off an indebtedness or to allow for deliveries on credit. Re-exportation of products is generally prohibited.

*Examples of Agreements.* As an example, the Argentinian agreement with Czechoslovakia may be cited. The current agreement dates from October 18, 1957, replacing an agreement of January 27, 1955, and is to be in effect for one year from November 5, 1957. The agreement is to be renewed automatically every year with the same provisions, unless cancelled with 90 days' notice. Argentina agrees to export, without quotas, hides, wool, oil cakes, fruit, dried fruit, preserves, and Czechoslovakia agrees to export, without quotas, iron, timber, diesel motors, glass and ceramics, and chemical products. Trade is to be at a value of $40 million per year and balanced except for a possible Czech line of credit. A swing credit of $3 million is specified and no re-exports are permitted. In previous agreements, the trade target had been lower and the products exchanged had been different. Argentina and Czechoslovakia have also negotiated some barter agreements which have been separate from the main trade agreement.

Brazil and East Germany signed a new trade agreement on September 23, 1958, to be in force for one year from that date. No targets were made known but Brazil will export coffee, cocoa, ores, vegetable oils, sisal, hides, fruit, and other tropical products, while East Germany will ship machinery and instruments, optical and photographic materials, chemical products, fertilizers, and engineering products. The agreement will be automatically renewed for equal periods unless cancelled.

On August 11, 1956, Uruguay and the Soviet Union negotiated their first governmental trade agreement, at which time a general treaty of commerce, friendship, and navigation was also signed. The agreement is to be in effect for two years beginning ten days after ratification and if not terminated in six months, the agreement will remain in force until terminated on three months' notice. The agreement has never been ratified by Uruguay, so that the previous non-governmental agreement, between the State Bank of the Soviet Union and the Uruguayan National Bank remains in effect. This latter agreement, specifying balanced trade and no quotas, calls upon Uruguay to export butter, beef, wool, mutton, and hides, and the Soviet Union agrees to export petroleum and petroleum products, coal, newsprint, iron and steel, chemicals, agricultural machinery, industrial equipment, and lumber. An agreement similar to the one proposed between the Soviet Union and Uruguay was signed September 12, 1955, between Czechoslovakia and Uruguay and was finally ratified by Uruguay in September, 1957. This three-year agreement was also accompanied by a commercial treaty providing for most-favored-nation treatment and calls for both countries to intensify and facilitate trade.

As an example of barter agreements, Chile, through the Sogeco Import-Export Company, agreed to trade $5 million worth of wool, cereals, wine, food, and fodder for $5 million worth of chemical and electric products and optical goods from the D.I.A., a semi-governmental East German organization in 1955 and 1956. Chile has also had barter agreements with Czechoslovakia. The most notable example of simple contract purchases has been the Soviet Union's contracts with Cuba. Each year since 1954 the Soviet Union has purchased Cuban sugar either through brokers in London and Havana or by sending specific missions to the Cuban Sugar Stabilization Institute. Payment for all deliveries has been in U.S. dollars under a normal commercial contract.

*Payments Agreements.* The payments agreements specify the financial arrangements by which the trade is conducted. They are frequently an integral part of the trade agreement, but occasionally are contained in a separate instrument, and usually have the same duration and renewal provisions as the trade agreement. The principal provisions define whether or not a convertible currency is to be employed and, if not, provide for the establishment of accounts in the appropriate financial institutions. The payments agreement specifies the currency unit of account and the credit provisions, be they swing, commercial, or long-term credit. The agreement also provides for the method of balancing accounts periodically and at the end of the agreement and for the correction and liquidation of seriously unbalanced accounts.

As is illustrated by Table 10, the network of payments agreements is substantially the same as that for trade agreements. It is not customary, however, to have a payments agreement for barter transactions, although in instances where a barter agreement is undertaken by countries which already have trade and payments agreements, the payments arrangements are sometimes utilized for the barter exchange as a matter of convenience. Despite the elaborate and somewhat complex payments system for Latin American trade with the Soviet Union and Eastern Europe, there is an incipient but definite maturing trend in Latin American trade toward cash dealings—a trend steadily fought by the Soviet-East European area. The conversion to convertible currencies in trade, already in progress

Table 10

Payments Agreements in Force in 1958 between Latin American
Countries and the Soviet Union and Eastern Europe*

| | Soviet Union | Bulgaria | Czechoslo- vakia | East Germany | Hungary | Poland | Rumania |
|---|---|---|---|---|---|---|---|
| Argentina | A,S,FC, LC | A,S,SC | A,S,SC,FC, LC | A,I | A,S,SC, FC,LC | A,S,SC, FC,LC | A,S,SC, FC,LC |
| Brazil | | | A | A,S | A,S | A,S | A,FC |
| Colombia | | | A,N | A,S,N | A,N | | |
| Mexico | | | A,S,FC | | | | |
| Paraguay | | | A,P,S, FC,I | | A,P,S, FC,I | A,P,S, I | |
| Uruguay | A,I | A,I | A,S,SC, FC | A,S,I | A,I | A,S,I | A,S,I |

Key:

    A  -  Agreement or clearing dollars
    P  -  Previous agreement - not in force in 1958
    S  -  Swing credit
    SC  -  Swing credit overdraft payable in convertible currency
    FC  -  Final balance payable in convertible currency
    LC  -  Line of credit by Soviet Union or Eastern Europe
    N  -  Non-governmental agreement only
    I  -  Interbank agreement

* No known agreements in 1958 for Bolivia, Chile, Costa Rica, Dominican Republic,
Ecuador, El Salvador, Guatemala, Haiti, Honduras, Nicaragua, Panama, Peru, and
Venezuela. Cuba is paid in U.S. dollars. Non-agreement trade is conducted in
transferable currencies, and agreements do not preclude the use of transferable
currencies.

Source: As in Table 9.

in Europe, would eventually lead to the abandonment of the payments
provisions of agreements, since, in general, their principal function
is to circumvent the use of foreign exchange.

*Agreement Accounts.* Relatively little trade is now openly on a
convertible currency basis, but in some of the payments agreements,
notably those of Uruguay, the Soviet Union and Eastern Europe
must export first, build up a credit balance, and then Uruguay will
issue import licenses up to the amount of the credit balance. In
several of the Uruguayan agreements, virtual cash is implied in pro-

visions which enable Uruguay to use a credit balance to pay third countries.

Most of the payments agreements remain, however, in "agreement dollars," meaning simply that the dollar is the unit of account and in general is not convertible. Soviet and East European exports build up a credit balance in the Latin American bank; Latin American exports build up credit balances in Soviet and East European banks. These accounts are periodically mutually cancelled. It is almost universal that the final balance at the end of the agreement will be settled in a convertible currency, and there is an increasing trend toward payment in a convertible currency in the event either one of the trading partners exceeds the limit of the swing credit.

The credit provisions universally allow for about 10% to 20% "swing," usually with no interest rate. In some instances, however, when the swing was used continuously in one direction an interest rate has been charged. Many of the payments agreements specify commercial credit for the purchase of capital goods from the East European countries at the customary interest rates. Long-term credit is usually not a part of the trade and payments agreements but is in a separate instrument, although the payments agreement outlines the financial provisions for the goods shipped under the line of credit.

The Czech-Argentinian payments agreement, having the same duration, renewal, and cancellation provisions as the previously mentioned trade agreement, specifies accounts in dollars in the Czech and Argentinian banks. Any excess of the 20% swing credit limit is payable on demand in dollars, gold, or other agreed currency. The balance remaining six months after expiration of the agreement is also payable in the same way.

The existing payments arrangement between the Soviet Union and Uruguay specifies that the account will be maintained in sterling in the Uruguayan Bank and that the latter country may debit the account for purchases or may pay in sterling. Soviet deposits (arising from its purchases) will be matched by Uruguayan import quotas (not necessarily imports). This agreement is only an inter-bank agreement. The still unratified inter-governmental payments agreement is more elaborate: accounts are to be maintained in dollars in the central bank of each country. In the event of a balance of $2 million for a period of one year, measures will be taken to liquidate. If negotiations do not take place within 60 days the balance must be liquidated in another 30 days in dollars, sterling, or other acceptable currency. Any balance over $4 million will be liquidated in 90 days. By agreement, sums in the account can be used to pay other countries. The final balance will also be liquidated in convertible currencies. The Uruguayan agreement with Czechoslovakia specifies that balances in excess of the swing credit limit, as well as the final balance, are to be liquidated by payment of U.S. dollars.

*World Price Base.* Barter transactions and contracts under trade agreements are negotiated from the base of world prices. Latin American countries export on the basis of the going export price of their products and their trading partners claim to do the same. Since, however, each transaction is unique and is the result of intergovernmental bargaining, there are occasional departures from world prices. Latin American countries are sometimes offered premium prices or are sold goods at prices lower than those in the world market. Depending on the bargaining strength of the trading partners and the incomparability of goods from different suppliers, particularly capital goods, prices are sometimes out of line the other way.

The negotiations of trade and payments agreements and barter transactions are conducted by diplomatic personnel or special delegations of the Soviet Union and Eastern European countries and either government officials or private individuals acting on behalf of Latin American trading organizations. In the large trading countries, such as Argentina, Brazil, and Uruguay, there are resident trading missions and these are often empowered to negotiate for other East European countries not represented in the country as well as to negotiate with other Latin American countries where no trading mission exists. Latin American countries seldom send trade delegations to the Soviet Union and Eastern Europe but sometimes use resident diplomatic personnel to negotiate on trade matters.

*Liberalization of Agreements.* It is apparent that trade and payments agreements between Latin America and the Soviet Union and Eastern Europe have undergone in recent years a gradual liberalization. Quotas have been abandoned in favor of commodity lists. Credit extension, by both sides, either in the form of commercial credit or the holding of balances, has become more common so that the strict bilateral balancing has been breaking down. In payments, the movement toward the use of convertible currencies is noticeable, with Uruguay in the lead.

The initiative for the liberalization comes from Latin America, which has not only been moving toward more liberalized trade with all of the world, but is also particularly anxious to avoid undue restrictions on its trade with the Soviet Union and Eastern Europe. The latter's performance under trade and payments agreements has not been wholly satisfactory to Latin America, as will be seen in the next section, and Latin America is anxious that bilateralism does not contribute to a worsening of its terms of trade.

The other aspects of commercial policy between the trading partners are largely in accordance with the standard practices of the countries involved. Under general treaties most-favored-nation treatment is accorded, although this has little meaning for the state-trading nations. Each country usually obligates itself to give all possible aid pertaining to the observance of the laws of each country, such as the collection of taxes and tariffs and the observance of rules and formalities of trade regulations. There is to be preferential treatment for the vessels of each country in the other country's ports. Thus, neither the commercial policy of Latin America nor of the Soviet Union and Eastern Europe is disturbed and their trade with one another takes place not only within the bounds of each country's accepted policy, but also within the framework of the special bilateral agreements.

*Trade Promotion.* The Soviet Union and Eastern Europe have conscientiously pursued a definite policy of trade expansion with Latin American countries. In general the former has come to the latter, often with elaborate economic overtures designed to entice Latin Americans into enlarged trade, sometimes accompanied by a large-scale propaganda barrage. The magnitude of these efforts is far beyond the scope and potential economic benefits of trade.

It is possible to separate out several strands in this policy. One is the offer of profitable trade. This takes the form of a promise to buy Latin American products at world market prices and to sell capital goods or such items as coal and petroleum at competitive prices or even at prices below the world market. Frequently these offers are in quite general terms, but on occasion a specific transaction is offered which is or may be beneficial to the Latin American country, if implemented satisfactorily.

*Credit.* The trade offers are made more attractive by the promise to extend credit to Latin American countries on favorable terms. The terms offered Latin America, however, have been somewhat more business-like than those offered in Asia, Africa, and the Middle East. The period ranges from three to twelve years, the usual offer being seven years. The interest rate, of course, is low on the longer-term credit. The Soviet Union has offered most of the long-term credit.

On commercial credit, however, East European countries, which have been most active in this field, have been charging the usual interest rate and employing standard repayment provisions. Credit offers in each case have been for capital goods, not for items such as petroleum, on current account. The loans are usable only in the country extending the credit and then only from the particular export organization which has the monopoly for the items covered by the line of credit. On some occasions, East European countries have entered bids on competitive projects, particularly where commercial credit only was involved. Czechoslovakia, for example, placed a bid on the expansion and modernization of Uruguay's telephone system.

Like the trade offers, the credit offers are often quite general and designed only as an initial approach, as in the case of Khrushchev's promise: "The Soviet government is ready to give all the assistance it can to Brazil's industrial advancement. We could reach agreement on the delivery of Soviet machines and equipment, on the dispatch of Soviet specialists to Brazil, and on the training of Brazilian specialists in the Soviet Union."[3] In other instances the offer is quite specific, covering the particular items which would be sold under the line of credit.

The official Soviet representative attending President Frondizi's inauguration extended a general offer of assistance to Argentina. In October, 1958, Argentina signed an agreement with the Soviet Union for a $100 million line of credit. The credit is earmarked for Argentine government purchase of petroleum industry equipment including electrical machinery and equipment, exploration and drilling equipment, including turbo-drills, seismograph equipment, motor vehicle transport equipment, pumps, and compressors. The credit is to be utilized within three years. Repayment will start three years after the first delivery and be completed in seven annual installments. Interest will be charged from the date of each shipment of Soviet goods at 2.5% per year. Contracts valued at $32 million had been signed by March, 1959. Argentinian deliveries will be wool, hides, quebracho extract, and other products.

Czech engineers are presently installing a coal washing plant at the state-owned Rio Turbio coal mines under a $2.1 million Czech credit. Agreement on this project was reached in July, 1955, the equipment arrived in early 1957, construction started in October, 1957, and the plant is to begin operations in October, 1959. Repayment of this credit will be 75% complete when the project goes into operation, with the remainder to be paid by 1961, so in effect this is commercial credit. Installed electric generating capacity at Rio Turbio will be significantly increased upon installation of two Czech turbo-generators of 6,000 KW capacity each, which were purchased in July, 1958, for $2 million on deferred payment terms up to 1963. Balances due after delivery will bear 6% interest. Delivery is scheduled within 19 months.

The largest Brazilian transaction was a contract in May, 1958, of the Brazilian Merchant Marine Commission with Poland for the purchase of 14 freighters valued at $24.1 million. Brazil is to supply in payment, over a period of several years, certain commodities including 300,000 bags of coffee valued at $15.7 million. Four of the ships are scheduled for delivery by May, 1960.

In April, 1958, Poland expressed interest in participating in a Minas Gerais state development program, outlining a proposal to equip a steel mill in the Para Poeba Valley. The governor, interested in the offer, asked the Poles to grant longer payment terms than were offered. The Polish delegation indicated that the project was too expensive for Poland to finance but stated that financing could be obtained from the Soviet Union, an example of the coordinated nature of Soviet economic efforts abroad.

*Other Promotion Techniques.* These two substantive elements of the Soviet and East European program—trade expansion and credit— are assiduously promoted by every means at their disposal. Trade delegations, both visiting and permanent, are constantly engaged in "selling" Latin America.

In mid-1958, for example, the Soviet commercial attache in Uruguay was reported to have tried to woo one of the leading importers and distributors of U.S. and British machinery. Exhibiting catalogs filled with a wide variety of machinery and automotive equipment, the Soviet official offered very attractive terms to the importer. He emphasized his willingness to meet all U.S. and British prices and promised prompt delivery of good quality merchandise. Of the sales price, only one-half would have to be turned over to the Soviet Union, the other 50% being reserved for advertising of the Soviet goods in Uruguay by the importer. The Uruguayan importer, however, turned down these proposals in order not to jeopardize his long-standing relations with U.S. and British firms.

Fairs and exhibits, particularly of industrial products, are used to acquaint Latin American buyers with Soviet and East European goods and are used as a platform to persuade officials, business leaders, and the people of the mutual benefits of trade. The first large Soviet industrial exhibit in Latin America was set up in Buenos Aires in May, 1955. Its impact was dulled somewhat by the Soviet debt to Argentina, but the exhibition did serve the Soviet purpose of impressing Argentinians with Soviet industrial prowess.

The Soviet Union and Czechoslovakia played a prominent role in the fifteenth anniversary exposition staged by the Argentine petroleum monopoly from December 13, 1957, to April 15, 1958. The Soviet exhibit, set up in an area renting for $100,000, included mobile drilling units, turbo-drills, and enough other oil field equipment to make it by far the most outstanding foreign entry in the entire exposition. The mass media in Latin America, such as the radio and the press, have given much free publicity to Soviet and East European activities and have also made available advertising time and space. The local Communist Party, of course, swings in behind any move to promote trade, not only by word of mouth, but in its publications and through sympathizers. The Soviet Union and Eastern Europe have gone out of the way to expand cultural exchanges with Latin American countries. High government spokesmen make public statements designed to assist in trade promotion. In their presentations, the Soviet Union and East European countries make it abundantly clear that they are anxious to trade, on a commercial basis, and that political and economic amity would be beneficial to both areas.

Technical assistance is another standard device employed by the Soviet Union and Eastern Europe to assist in trade promotion and exercise influence. Most technical assistance, however, is an adjunct of a specific project and is seldom separated from a plant or machinery and equipment from the Soviet-East European area. There have been relatively few technicians from the Soviet Union and Eastern Europe in Latin America. In 1958 Argentina was host to about 45 technical experts and there were a few in Chile.  Since, however, there have been few large-scale installations of Soviet and East European equipment, the need for technicians has been modest.  Latin America, having observed experiences elsewhere, is wary of the political and ideological influence of Soviet-East European technical teams.

\*       \*       \*

In sum, Soviet and East European commercial policies in Latin America share most of the characteristics of its policies elsewhere in the world—bilateral balancing of trade under inter-governmental trade and payments agreements, and must be characterized as fundamentally similar to the reactionary policies used in the 1930's in Europe.  Because of this unsatisfactory policy framework, Latin American countries have insisted upon a moderate amendment of the strict bilateral form, increasingly urging multilateral payments.

The willingness of Latin American countries on the one hand and the Soviet-East European area on the other to continue trading and in some cases even to expand trade constitutes at least some indirect evidence that the performance of the trading partners has been minimally acceptable. It does not follow, however, that these trading partners have by any means been satisfied with trade and do not seek substantial improvement in their relations. Indeed, there is considerable evidence that Latin America in particular has been dissatisfied, and some of these countries have suspended or threatened to suspend trade if Soviet and East European performance did not improve.

In the last half of 1956 Argentina suspended hide shipments because of unsatisfactory commercial relations. Uruguay has also suspended shipments. Brazil denounced its agreement with Poland in 1956 because trade was more favorable to Poland than to Brazil. Gustavo Storm, president of the Paraguayan central bank said, in calling for a re-examination of trade agreements with the bloc (which was a prelude to their cancellation): "The present accords with countries behind the Iron Curtain not only did not give the results that some people childishly expected but showed that even according to the economic point of view, these accords were unsatisfactory." (*New York Herald Tribune*, April 13, 1956).

Expressions of dissatisfaction have recurred periodically, down to the present time. On April 14, 1959, Mr. Walter Muller, Chilean Ambassador to the United States, declared that the Soviet trade offensive in Latin America was a "fizzle." Some political parties in Latin America, he stated, had made "great propaganda out of Russian trade offers" but so far "the offers were all talk and no action." (*New York Times*, April 15, 1959.)

The principal element which has piqued the Soviet Union and Eastern Europe is their belief that the United States and other Western powers influence or control the commercial and economic policies of Latin American countries.[1] The Soviet-East European area frequently attributes to this alleged fact its own inability to expand trade and negotiate trade agreements. The Soviet Union and Eastern Europe have made known their preference both for bilateralism and state

34

trading and are deeply chagrined at Latin America's constant pressure
for multilateral trade and insistence on private trading.[2]  The reluctance of Latin countries to purchase sufficient goods to fulfill the
targets specified in the agreements or to offset their sales, the Soviet
Union and Eastern Europe attribute to non-commercial reasons,
particularly pressure from the United States and Europe.  The Soviet
Union and Eastern Europe are unwilling to accept any of the responsibility for the low level of trade.  Of the trade which has taken place,
however, the Soviet Union and Eastern Europe have had no criticisms
as to price, quality, and terms of the transactions.   *1100577*

Latin American judgment has been somewhat more critical.  These
criticisms involve not only the trade itself but also the apparatus by
which trade is conducted.  There are four central issues on which the
Soviet Union and Eastern Europe must be regarded as having performed unsatisfactorily from the point of view of their trading partners.
They are: (1) the bilateral framework of the trade and state trading
methods, (2) pricing of products and the terms of trade, (3) competition, and (4) the obvious political nature of the trade from the Soviet
and East European point of view.

*Bilateralism and State Trading.*  Doing business with a state
trading country automatically puts the Latin American countries
at a disadvantage, even presuming the best of intentions and a desire
to engage in mutually beneficial trade on the part of the state trading
nation.  Private interests, which dominate Latin American trade,
are in a relatively weaker bargaining position in dealing with state
trading organizations, not only because of sheer size, but also because
of the monopoly characteristics of the latter.  Unlike "tied" contracts
and loans by Western countries, in trading with a state trader the
Latin American country must conduct its business not with a group
of competing enterprises in the same line of selling or buying, but
rather with a single governmental organization.  If Argentina wishes
to buy oil, it must do business with one trading unit and that one
only; in selling hides, it must bargain with another single unit only.

Thus, trade with the Soviet Union and Eastern Europe takes on
many of the aspects of a governmental operation.  It tends to
become inflexible once the state trading organization has received
its instructions and suffers from bureaucratization and red tape.
There is no such thing as the "normal" course of business.  Each
transaction becomes a major operation, from the first gentle hints,

to lengthy negotiations, and, finally, to the conclusion of complicated contracts. Each transaction is unique. Needless to say, there are many shortcomings in such a process of negotiating trade. The Soviet Union had indicated a desire to purchase all of Argentina's mutton exports in 1957. But when it came time to negotiate a contract, the Soviet Union had lost interest, aggravating Argentina's marketing problem and forcing the sale of the mutton at lower prices elsewhere.

The framework of bilateralism in itself is objectionable to Latin American countries. While, as an area, Latin America has been one of the leading practitioners of bilateralism, dating back to the early 1930's when the scheme was first introduced into modern commercial policy, Latin America has increasingly tended to regard its products as cash products—a justifiable presumption—and in the postwar period has gradually moved toward multilateral trade. This movement has accelerated in the past three years because Latin America's chief markets are in convertible or transferable currency areas—in Europe and North America—and these areas are also the principal suppliers of Latin American imports. On the other hand, the Soviet Union which before the Second World War had in general accepted multilateral trading methods, now insists upon bilateral trade and payments agreements and bilateral balancing of trade. Only under considerable pressure will the Soviet Union trade without a highly specific agreement in convertible currencies.

The practice of bilateral balancing of trade forces Latin American countries into making sufficient purchases from their bilateral trading partners to cover their sales, regardless of whether or not such purchases represent the best possible buy at the time. Indeed, the agreements, in specifying a certain level of sales to the Soviet Union and Eastern European countries do not necessarily assure that Latin American countries get the best price for their products. Prices of both imports and exports are negotiated at a later time in specific contract discussions. Bilateral trade in general is uneconomic and does not result in the greatest possible economic benefits from trade. Latin America has on some occasions been faced with circumstances in which bilateral trade, however, is better than no trade at all and the Soviet Union and Eastern Europe have capitalized on those situations. Latin America has not been particularly pleased by this somewhat opportunistic attitude.

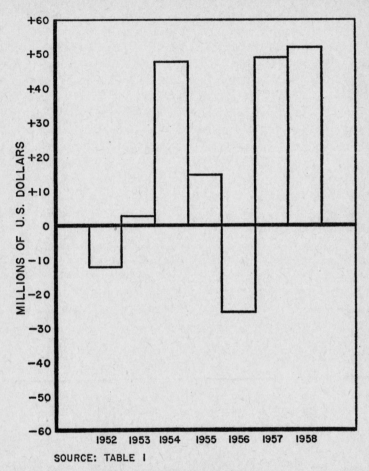

SOURCE: TABLE I

CHART 2   LATIN AMERICAN TRADE BALANCES
WITH THE SOVIET UNION AND EASTERN EUROPE

*Problem of Imbalances.* Latin America has had difficulty keeping
the bilateral accounts balanced, as can be seen in Chart 2. These
countries are knowledgeable traders with long years of experience in
handling their products. In general, when they agree to export, they
do it, with alacrity and accuracy. On the other hand, the Soviet
Union is an inexperienced trader; Eastern Europe is better, but even
so, products are not as readily available, less is known about what
is available, and deliveries are not prompt. The result is that there
has been a chronic tendency for Latin America to run an export
surplus. This is apparent in the annual trade data in the previous
chapter, but would be even more evident on a monthly or quarterly
basis. Latin American countries are constantly under pressure to
buy more, even when they do not know what to buy or how to buy
it and they are constantly putting pressure on the Soviet Union and
Eastern Europe to make more goods available and deliver what has
already been ordered.

The imbalances have been most serious in Argentina and everywhere the export surpluses have been an annoyance. One device
has been to use the balance by paying higher prices to induce the bloc
country to export. For example, Uruguay has purchased coal at a
price markedly above the world market price in an attempt to utilize
some of the balances that have accumulated from the shipment of
wool to Poland. Rubles and East European currencies have also
been sold on occasion at a discount, sometimes by as much as 50%,
in order to use up some of the balances. Both Brazil and Uruguay
have found this course necessary in some instances. Importers willing
to take these currencies were provided import licenses which enabled
them to import from third countries, which were paid in the over-
valued currencies.

While individual importers may have gained in the use of the
bilateral balances, the country was not able to import either the kind
or the quantity of goods called for by the undiscounted value of the
balances. This practice, along with delays, administrative obstacles,
inordinate negotiating time, and other time and resource consuming
activities involved in trading with the Soviet Union and Eastern
Europe engender in fact an increase in the import price of the goods
which Latin America does buy and hence a worsening in the terms
of trade with respect to the Soviet Union and Eastern Europe. These
complications also act as a depressant on the level of trade.

The apparent chronic inability of both sides to attain the targets specified in trade agreements has been another disturbing element, particularly to Latin America. In Soviet agreements with Argentina, Brazil, and Uruguay, the Soviet Union, between 1953 and 1956, exported 49% of the value of the agreement targets and imported 47% of the value of the agreement targets. Eastern European agreements with the same countries display better performance, but still Eastern Europe exported only 60% and imported 62% of the targets specified in the agreements.

*Argentina's Balances.* Argentina allowed its balances with the Soviet-East European area to accumulate over a period of years and finally, in desperation, in January, 1958, sent a special mission to the Soviet Union and several East European countries. The mission, which became known as the "Ondarts Mission" after the Argentinian Under-secretary of Commerce and Industry, entered into contracts for the importation of various items, but even so, the Argentinian orders were not able to absorb all of the balances on hand. The mission did sign contracts for $27 million in capital goods, mainly for goods from Czechoslovakia, leaving, however, as much as $15 million still standing to Argentina's credit.

The Soviet Union and Argentina agreed to trade $75 million each way and the Soviet Union agreed to loan Argentina an additional $30 million in August, 1953. In 1954 Argentina exported $45.6 million and imported $28.9 million. It took Argentina two years to export $75.3 million and the Soviet Union required two years to export $68.9 million. During the second year another agreement was signed calling for $50 million in trade each way; the credit, none of which had been used, was reduced to $4 million. By the end of 1958 imports and exports of Argentina *vis-à-vis* the Soviet Union were both still less than the $125 million negotiated in 1953 and 1955. This is not an isolated example. In almost every instance trade fell short, usually on both sides, of fulfilling the terms of the trade agreement. Latin America, of course, could easily have fulfilled the agreements, but did not dare to in the face of almost certain unusable balances.

\*　　\*　　\*

One of the most important obstacles to expanded trade and one particularly difficult for Latin Americans to understand has been the absence of knowledge of the details about the supplier's goods, prices, quality and performance characteristics, and delivery capabilities. There is increasing advertising in the Latin American press, and trade delegations are reasonably well-informed, but there is an inordinate gap between the desire to import a product, placing an order, and the delivery of the product. In many instances, Latin Americans simply do not know what is available. Items that are known to be produced and items that have been advertised and publicized at trade fairs do not seem to be available. Placing an order results either in an initial rebuff or after some delay the order is returned with the indication that the item is not available for export.

*Prices and the Terms of Trade.* Since Soviet and East European currencies are not convertible, and in fact not even transferable among themselves, there is no necessity for prices in these countries to bear any relationship either to world market prices generally or to opportunity costs within the area. The centralized planning system of the Soviet Union and later of Eastern Europe has, in fact, distorted the internal price system of each country out of all recognition. These pricing systems do not resemble each other at the official or any other exchange rate and show no relationship to world market prices. The Soviet Union imports Cuban sugar, for instance, at an exchange rate, in terms of Soviet domestic prices, 34 times the official exchange rate. In 1958 crude oil was shipped to Argentina at an exchange rate 5.5 times the official rate if the Soviet domestic crude price is used. The Soviet-East European area simply has no independent pricing policy. Its trade is basically parasitical, depending wholly on the operations of world markets to perform the price setting function.

There is, however, something fundamentally wrong with the concept of a separate and independent, yet price-dependent market. The fact is that no market, even if insulated by nonconvertibility, can be really separate and independent. Stalin's dictum on "parallel" markets is factually incorrect and theoretically unsound.[3] The Soviet Union and Eastern Europe are a part of one world market. Their supplies, placed on the export market, add to the total goods available. Their demands, felt in import markets, are a portion of the total world demand. Indeed, the Soviet Union has bragged that its Cuban sugar purchases contributed to the maintenance of sugar prices, even though the Soviet Union paid slightly less than other purchasers. The amounts of goods these countries market and purchase help determine the total volume of goods exchanged and the prices at which they are exchanged. With a fixed demand, an increased supply of Soviet and

East European goods on the market will put pressure on prices, which will tend to fall. With a fixed supply, an increased demand by these countries will also tend to raise prices as they bid against other buyers for the limited amount of goods.

*Use of World Prices.* The Soviet Union and Eastern Europe—a part of the world market but without a pricing system—accept the world market as a guide. Indeed, they seem to be proud of this and have even embodied this principle in some of their trade agreements. As a matter of mechanical operation, they can trade at world market prices, but as a matter of fact, their imports and exports affect the world market price. When they offer a country trade at world market prices, at first it appears that the terms of trade of their trading partner would improve, since the latter's products would remain either unsold or sold at a lower price in the absence of the "world market price" deal.

This innocence is quickly dispelled when it is remembered that the Soviet and East European demand, as a part of world demand, has in fact tended to raise the world market price of their trading partner's exports. Yet the product is sold at the world market price which prevails in the absence of the Soviet-East European demand. At the same time the Soviet Union and Eastern Europe are selling at the world market price, but their new supply tends to lower the price of these exports. A Latin American country is offered the products at the world market price as though the Soviet-Eastern Europe supply did not exist. Thus, on both ends, the terms of trade tend to worsen for Latin America—its import prices are higher than they would have been if the world price had taken into account its trading partners' supply, and its export prices are lower. While apparently these terms of trade seem to be the same as the rest of its trade and may be numerically the same, they are lower than they would have been had not the trade been isolated and protected within a framework of bilateralism. Only under the shelter of non-convertibility, bilateral agreements, and lack of knowledge about Soviet and East European export supply and import demand can this fiction be maintained.

Just how much worse the terms of trade with the Soviet Union and Eastern Europe are than the rest of the Latin American trade is difficult to say. The more inelastic the demand for Latin American products, the greater would have been the price effect of the new

Soviet-East European demand. The more inelastic the supply of Soviet and East European goods, the greater the price consequences also. Furthermore, the greater the Soviet and East European supply and demand, the greater the price and terms of trade effect. Since trade has been small and despite the relatively high inelasticity of some Latin American products, it is unlikely that dependent characteristics of Soviet-East European trade have had a serious effect on overall Latin American terms of trade. But it must be remembered that this aspect as well as the sheltered aspects of the trade imply that the Soviet Union and Eastern Europe do not face Western competition in exports and provide a setting within which Soviet and East European terms of trade are improved at the expense of Latin America.

*Pricing Policy.* The pricing practices of the Soviet Union and Eastern Europe have conformed reasonably closely to their stated principles. Most goods have been exchanged at the prevailing world market prices or at a negotiated price for both imports and exports which had as its starting point the world market price of the product. This means, of course, that Latin American exports have been underpriced and Soviet and East European exports have been overpriced, even without considering the fact that the superior bargaining power of state trading agencies enables them to dominate price determination. There have been, however, relatively few instances of price gouging, but this factor has not been wholly absent. In mid-1957 Argentina purchased Polish coal at $31.50 per ton when U.S. coal was being laid down in Europe at $22.50 per ton. This discrepancy derived in part from Argentina's desire to forestall the accumulation of further Polish balances. In some cases, the Soviet Union and Eastern Europe have offered premium prices for Latin American products or have sold at prices lower than those prevailing in the world market. This development, of course, can take place without adversely affecting the terms of trade and in instances where it has happened it serves merely as a partial redress for the automatic worsening in Latin American terms of trade.

Another factor serving to dampen Latin American enthusiasm for trade with the Soviet-East European area is the generally poor quality of Soviet and East European goods and the absence of adequate servicing and spare parts for equipment, which in effect increases the import price of the product. This problem has been particularly acute in instances where Soviet or East European goods have been found defective. Argentina, for example, discovered that "Skoda" trucks purchased from Czechoslovakia did not measure up to the rated capacity claimed for them in Czech advertising. Although faulty motors and cooling systems rendered about 1,000 of these trucks useless, Czechoslovakia refused to make any restitution. The incident has become a *cause celebre*, with the Argentine Chamber of Deputies in July, 1958, passing a resolution demanding a full report on the purchase of the Czech trucks.

Similarly, defects have bobbed up in steel cables, pneumatic hammers, power shovels, and motor compressors supplied to Argentina by the Soviet Union. Many of these items have demonstrated an amazingly brief working life and much less sturdiness and efficiency than their rated capacities called for. Steel cables have snapped under loads well below their rated strength; weak pistons and valves in pneumatic hammers have had to be replaced after only three months' service; new motors, springs, and other parts were required in four Soviet-manfactured power shovels after less than one year of service; motor clutches and compressor repairs were needed for six motor compressors within 500 hours after being put into operation. Brazil returned as defective a whole shipload of lathes to Poland, a factor influencing the Brazilian denunciation of its trade agreement with Poland in 1956.

To Latin American countries long familiar with the standards of quality in goods from the United States and Western Europe, such problems as those experienced by Argentina are almost incomprehensible. A greater wariness is developing in Latin America against blind acceptance of Soviet-East European claims of performance for equipment, and new demands are being made for assurances of adequate replacement parts and better quality goods before orders are placed.

Other characteristics of the trade have also affected the terms of trade, nearly all in the direction of weakening the Latin American position. Holding nonconvertible, noninterest-bearing balances costs Latin America and amounts to the same thing as an increase in the import price or a lowering of the export price. Delays in delivery, bureaucratic ineptitudes, lengthy negotiations, complicated bookkeeping and contractual arrangements, and other factors also tend to worsen Latin American terms of trade. Poor quality goods and the lack of adequate servicing and spare-parts have become increasingly disturbing.  Selling balances at a discount, as mentioned earlier, adds to Latin American costs.  These latter attributes of the trade have probably had a serious effect on Latin America's terms of trade, all negative, and have substantially reduced, perhaps even eliminated, the gains from trade which Latin America expected.

*Soviet-East European Competition.*  In a later section the extent to which the Soviet-East European area and Latin America are complementary and competitive will be examined in some detail. Here it is necessary to point out that Soviet and East European competition in products which Latin America also markets has been a distinctly disturbing factor.  The Soviet Union and Eastern Europe are competitors with Latin America in petroleum, cotton, wheat, tin, and other metals.

*Soviet Tin Exports.*  Soviet exports of tin have been the principal problem.  The Soviet Union exported 2,100 tons in 1955, having imported 16,900 tons from mainland China that year.  In the next year, Soviet imports from China were 15,700 and exports were 3,300. In 1957, however, the Soviet Union exported 18,300 tons and imported (from China) 22,000 tons.  In 1958 the Soviet Union again exported about 18,000 tons.  In September, 1958, the International Tin Council ran out of funds with which to buy tin for the buffer stock at the prevailing price, and the tin stabilization agreement collapsed.  The price of tin went down by more than 15%.

In Latin America, Bolivia was the hardest hit and that country has estimated a loss of at least $20 million as a result of what it calls "Soviet dumping."  It is difficult to assess this charge against a state trading country, since internal costs and prices bear no systematic relationship to world prices.  It is interesting to note, however, that the Soviet imports of 22,000 tons in 1957 were at a unit import value of 8,278 rubles per ton.  The unit export value was 8,226 rubles per ton.[4]  Thus, technically, the Soviet Union sold the tin at slightly below its own ruble cost, while simultaneously acquiring $37.6 million in transferable currency, equal to about two-thirds of the assets of the tin stabilization fund, of which the Soviet Union was not a member.

The tin price did not stay low for long.  Its recovery, however, left the Soviet Union substantially the gainer.  In November, 1958, the Soviet Union signified that it would be willing to abide by the price and quantity stabilization plans of the tin council.  In January,

1959, the International Tin Council announced that the Soviet Union, still not a member, intended to reduce shipments in 1959 to 13,700 tons to non-Communist countries. As recently as March, 1959, however, Soviet offers to Argentinian buyers shaded the London price by 8%.

It is unlikely that Soviet tin sales were undertaken in an effort to hurt Bolivia and other tin producers. It is probable that the tin was acquired from China in the latter's effort to reduce its very large import surplus with the Soviet Union in 1957. Having no need for the metal, but needing sterling, the Soviet Union sold the tin, disregarding the international ramifications of the act.

*Politics and Trade.* While politics has not always entered directly into trade negotiations or into the implementation of trade transactions, it constantly hovers in the background in the form of the missionary zeal of trade delegates and diplomats and statements from Soviet and East European government officials. Amicable political and economic relations are nearly always coupled together, sometimes in quite general terms, but on many occasions in the form of reluctance to trade in the absence of diplomatic recognition and relations. Brazil is keenly aware of the coupling of trade to diplomatic relations; the Soviet Union seldom misses an opportunity to relate "normalization" of diplomatic relations to expanded trade. Latin Americans are, of course, uncomfortably aware of the political sensitivity of trade with the Soviet Union and Eastern Europe and some tend to be resentful of continuous reminders.

\* \* \*

In sum, trade performance by the Soviet Union and Eastern Europe has been far from satisfactory to Latin America. The chief sources of complaint derive from the restrictive bilateral framework and state trading, in which Latin America has tended to have an export surplus and whose trade targets have chronically been underfulfilled, the fact that the terms of trade of this portion of trade have been unfavorable to Latin America, the unavailability and quality of goods, the competition from Soviet-East European products, and the political overtones of the trade.

The gross national product of Latin America in 1958 was approximately $55 billion, about one-third that of the Soviet Union and less than one-eighth that of the United States. More than 80% of the product originated in seven countries—Argentina, Brazil, Chile, Colombia, Cuba, Mexico, and Venezuela. Nearly one-half originated in two countries—Brazil and Argentina. Brazil's product is about 20% greater than that of Argentina and approximates the combined product of all Latin American countries except Argentina, Colombia, Mexico, and Venezuela.[1]

The growth of total Latin American gross product in constant prices on a per capita basis was approximately 3% per year between 1945 and 1951, but it halted in 1952 and 1953. In 1954 growth resumed its previous pace until 1956, a year in which there was relatively little growth. In the period 1950-1955, gross product grew at 2.2% per year. In 1957 growth was 2.4%. In 1958 again there was little growth. If Venezuela is excluded, the 1950-1955 growth was 1.9%, in 1956 there was no growth, and in 1957 growth was 1.9%.

Individual countries fared differently. Per capita growth was strongest in Brazil, Colombia, Mexico, and Venezuela, while proportionately less progress has been made in Argentina, Chile, and Cuba, although Cuba's growth in 1956 and 1957 was notable. Some countries which have rapid population growth made significant gains. Colombia, which until 1956 and 1957, was making considerable progress, is one of the countries with the highest population growth. On the other hand, countries with low population growth rates in some instances did not grow rapidly, as in the case of Argentina.

The principal characteristic of Latin American growth has been its unevenness. In one year a particularly good harvest or fortunate terms of trade may result in a very substantial gain in total real product, a favorable balance of trade, and budgetary surplus. The next year, under reverse conditions, there may be no growth, or perhaps even a deterioration. Only a few countries which have relatively diversified economies, such as Mexico, can maintain a reasonably stable growth rate.

In recent years between 79% and 83% of total gross national

product has been consumed. In 1957, for example, consumption was 81% of the total and during the last four years, consumption has taken 81% to 82%. Thus, investment, running from 17% to 21% of total product, has resulted in a growth in capital stock of more than one-third since 1950, with a nearly constant capital-output ratio. Domestic savings have provided more than 90% of the total investment in the area. Foreign investment, nonetheless, has played an important role in several countries, particularly Argentina, Brazil, Mexico, Venezuela, and some others.

Between 1945 and 1955, while absolute gross product rose an average of 5.1% per year, manufacturing grew even faster, while mining and agriculture grew at a lesser pace, agriculture having been the slowest growing sector. In 1957 the trend was interrupted and agriculture made impressive gains, both absolutely and relative to other sectors. Industry made some progress but lost ground relatively, while construction gained ground. Mining has been a persistently growing sector. In 1957 agriculture claimed a 23.3% share of total product. Along with industry whose share was 19.7%, government with 7.4%, transportation and communications with 8.4%, and other services with 15.6%, agriculture grew more slowly than total product. Mining with a share of 5.4%, construction with a 3.5%, and trade and finance with 16.8% grew more rapidly.

*Worsening Situation.* The economic position of Latin America deteriorated seriously in 1957 - 1958. Except in a few countries, such as Mexico, 1958 was one of the worst years since the Great Depression for the area as a whole. Growth continued to a very limited extent, but the major problems besetting the area became more acute. Inflation was serious in many countries, particularly Argentina and Brazil. Some currencies were depreciated. The trade surplus of 1956 was turned to serious deficits in 1957 and 1958 and governments ran large deficits. In some countries stocks of primary products accumulated to an alarming degree in 1958. Despite an inflow of $1.3 billion in United States capital in 1957, concentrated, however, primarily in the Venezuelan petroleum industry, little change took place in the output composition or export mix of Latin American countries.

Large-scale financial assistance continued in 1958. The Export-Import Bank loaned $447.4 million. The International Monetary Fund and private financial institutions also extended loans. In spite of all of the assistance, Latin American countries pared down imports to essential items, and some undertook "austerity" programs. The terms of trade of Latin America deteriorated, as import prices remained substantially the same and export prices continued to decline. Primary products continued to dominate Latin American export earnings and little progress was made in diversification. All in all, the Latin American economic and trading position at the beginning of 1959 was as acute as it had been at any time since 1937.

*Principal Problems.*  Three closely interrelated problems, and a host of lesser, but by no means minor difficulties dominate the economic position and prospects of Latin America.  These are: (1) the need for economic development, particularly in terms of growth rates substantially in excess of the rates of population growth, with emphasis on diversification toward manufacturing, import substitutes, and new export products, (2) the chronic and serious inflation and inflationary pressures and all of the problems causing the inflation, attendant on it, and resulting from it, and (3) a structure of foreign trade characterized by heavy dependence upon a relatively few primary products which are especially vulnerable to wide price variations in the world market.  There are many less pervasive problems, including existing or potential political instability in some countries, the absence of sufficient domestic savings, an extremely skewed distribution of income, extreme poverty in some countries, restrictive policies both in foreign trade and in the domestic economy, and the need to improve the efficiency of nearly all sectors of the economy.

*Population, Per Capita Incomes, and Economic Growth.*  The total population of Latin America is slightly less than 180 million people. More than 60% of the population, however, is in three countries— Mexico, Argentina, and Brazil—and Brazil alone has approximately one-third of the total population.  The land area of Latin America, however, is so huge that the density of population is less than the density in most other areas of the world, including the United States, Western and Eastern Europe, and Asia.

Nearly all of Latin America is experiencing a population explosion. The population of the area will double in slightly more than a generation if present birth and death rates continue.  The average rate of population growth for the entire area is 2.45% per year.  Six South American countries, including Argentina, Brazil, and Colombia, which are the most highly populated countries in South America, have been growing more slowly than the average. All of the Central American countries except Haiti have been growing more rapidly than the average. In comparison with other areas of the world, Latin America's rate of population growth is very high. The United States is growing at 1.8% per year; West and East European countries are growing at between 0.5% and 2.0%; Soviet growth is less than 2.0% per year. Table 11 indicates Latin American population growth.

The most serious implication of the rate of population growth in Latin America is that it dictates the rate of effective economic growth. While per capita income figures are to some extent misleading, in that they conceal the range and dispersion of incomes and give no indication of the actual or potential economic contribution of the members of the population, they are in time series form a useful measure of the rate of net economic progress. In 1955, the most recent year for which data are available, the average income for Latin America as a whole was about $300 per person per year as is shown

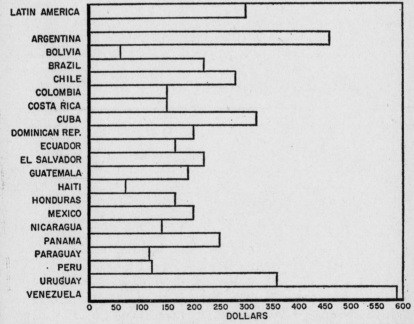

SOURCE: *COMPARATIVE STATISTICS ON THE AMERICAN REPUBLICS,* WTIS 58-3, COMMERCE DEPT. 1958.

**CHART 3    PER CAPITA INCOME IN LATIN AMERICA IN 1955**

in Chart 3, implying that 1958 per capita income was no more than $320 per year.

The most prosperous countries, those with per capita incomes above the average, are Venezuela, Argentina, Uruguay, and Cuba. On the other hand, a few countries have extremely low per capita incomes; Costa Rica, Nicaragua, Peru, and Paraguay have per capita incomes below $150 per year and Haiti and Bolivia have per capita incomes of less than $75 a year. These figures stand in stark contrast to the per capita income of the United States of more than $2,000 per year.

On the basis of the rate of population growth, the Latin American economies must grow at the rate of 2.5% per year consistently in order to maintain the present levels of per capita income, with, of course, variations from country to country. In the postwar period, growth has been sufficient to overcome this population barrier. Between 1950 and 1955 per capita growth in gross product was 2.2% per year; in 1955-1956 it was only 0.4%, but it picked up to 2.4% in 1956-1957. Thus, not only has Latin America grown very substantially in the postwar period, but this growth has been almost sufficient to maintain the relative position of Latin America with respect to the United States and West European powers. Indeed, in some cases, some Latin American countries have grown at rates which compare favorably with the growth rates claimed by the Soviet Union. Venezuela has consistently grown at high rates—9.7% in 1955, 8.0% in 1956, and 9.2% in 1957. Cuba has also made substantial progress, as have Mexico and Brazil. (Table 11.)

*Erratic Growth.* Characteristic, however, of Latin American growth is the wide variation from year to year. Depending on the crop, the terms of trade, and progress on various aspects of investment, the rate of growth, on a per capita basis, may well be more than 7% in one year, less than one-half that the next year, and at other times conceivably even negative. There is little possibility of avoiding instability in growth rates until Latin American economies become sufficiently diversified, with a broad enough base in all the lines of economic activity so that disaster in one sector or in one aspect of the economy does not stall growth for the entire system.

Assuming the rate of population growth remains the same as it is now, it will take Latin America 100 years to attain the per capita income the United States now enjoys, if Latin America is able to maintain an advancement in per capita income of about 2% per year. A doubling of per capita incomes in Latin America would take

Table 11

Growth Rates of Population and Gross Product

in Selected Latin American Countries

(per cent per year)

| | Annual Rate of Population Growth | Annual Rate of Per Capita Gross Product Growth | | |
|---|---|---|---|---|
| | (1953-1956) | 1955 | 1956 | 1957 |
| Argentina | 1.9 | 2.1 | -2.0 | 1.1 |
| Brazil | 2.4 | 1.7 | -0.3 | 4.1 |
| Chile | 2.6 | 0.4 | -5.2 | -2.2 |
| Colombia | 2.2 | 4.1 | -0.1 | 0.0 |
| Peru | 2.2 | 1.6 | -0.2 | 0.1 |
| Venezuela | 3.1 | 6.6 | 3.9 | 6.1 |
| Mexico | 2.9 | 6.6 | 1.6 | 1.6 |
| Cuba | -- | 1.5 | 7.1 | 6.1 |
| Latin America | 2.45 | 3.3 | 0.4 | 2.4 |
| Latin America (excluding Venezuela) | -- | 2.9 | 0.0 | 1.9 |

Source: Population data from International Statistical Yearbook, United
Nations, 1958.  Data for Costa Rica 3.9, Dominican Republic 3.4,
El Salvador 3.4, Guatemala 3.1, Haiti 1.2, Honduras 3.0,
Nicaragua 3.4, Panama 2.7, Bolivia 1.2, Ecuador 2.7, Paraguay 2.9,
and Uruguay 1.5 per cent.  Economic growth data from Economic
Survey of Latin America, 1957, Economic Commission for Latin
America, New York, 1959.

place in 35 years under these circumstances.  It is probable that if
some countries in Latin America were to grow at 4% to 5% per year
in per capita income and further to make sufficient strides toward

diversification that the growth rate would smooth out considerably. Argentina, Brazil, Mexico, and Chile, and other countries have the resource base for such development, and some can perhaps grow even more rapidly. Other countries—some of the small Central American states and a few of the South American countries—where the rate of economic growth has been slower, where resources are not adequate, and where the rate of population growth has been faster than the average—may have difficulty in maintaining even a 1% increase in per capita income per year.

*Requirements for Development.* Even though several Latin American countries possess the economic resources necessary for substantial and rapid economic development, thereby relieving the population pressure and providing for stable increases in per capita incomes, there is no automatic assurance that such development will take place. It certainly will not take place simply because the leadership of those countries wants it or thinks the importance of the country deserves it. It will take place only with wise policies, a willingness to sacrifice now for the future, and with economic organizations suited to the needs of the country.

Not only must there be sufficient investment, but it must be directed toward its most productive uses. Despite the efforts of Latin American countries to increase the volume of domestic savings, little progress has been made in recent years toward increasing the rate of savings. Many countries remain in the grips of the "vicious circle of poverty"—not enough income for people to save. This condition means in turn that relatively little investment is possible by which income can be increased. Furthermore, it is likely that the marginal propensity to consume of the higher income brackets is quite high, accomplished in part by importing high-cost consumer durables, which not only decreases savings and hence investment, but also uses up scarce foreign exchange which might be used for development purposes.

Inflationary domestic economic policies further discourage savings. The net result is relatively little domestic savings—inadequate to meet the requirements of growth at desired levels—and no great prospects that savings will increase substantially in the near future, at least relative to income. Foreign loans and investment have been, are, and will continue to be required if Latin America hopes to continue to make progress. Despite some antipathy to foreign investment, however, several countries, including Argentina, Brazil, Mexico, and Venezuela, have worked out methods by which foreign capital can operate effectively and the individual country can benefit economically without any accompanying infringement of its national sentiments.

*Inflation.*  Inflation has extracted a heavy penalty from many

Table 12

Cost of Living Indices in Selected Latin American Countries

(1953 = 100)

|  | 1952 | 1954 | 1955 | 1956 | 1957 | 1958* |
|---|---|---|---|---|---|---|
| Argentina | 96 | 104 | 117 | 132 | 165 | 275 |
| Bolivia | 50 | 223 | 402 | 1,120 | 2,410 | 2,870 |
| Brazil | 82 | 118 | 145 | 172 | 206 | 265 |
| Chile | 80 | 173 | 302 | 471 | 627 | 843 |
| Colombia | 93 | 109 | 108 | 115 | 132 | 155 |
| Mexico | 102 | 105 | 122 | 128 | 135 | 155 |
| Nicaragua | 89 | 108 | 123 | 118 | 114 | 110 |
| Paraguay | 58 | 120 | 148 | 180 | 209 | 226 |
| Peru | 92 | 105 | 110 | 116 | 125 | 139 |
| Uruguay | 94 | 112 | 122 | 130 | 149 | 182** |

*December, 1958                                    **October, 1958

Source:  International Financial Statistics, March, 1959.  The increases for Costa Rica, Cuba, Dominican Republic, Ecuador, El Salvador, Guatemala, Haiti, Honduras, Panama, and Venezuela were all less than 20 per cent between 1953 and the end of 1958.

Latin American economies, particularly Argentina, Bolivia, Brazil, Chile, and Paraguay. The Central American states generally have had a much more modest inflation. In Bolivia a runaway inflation slowed up substantially in 1958, but in Argentina the inflation has become more severe in 1957 and 1958. Brazil and Chile have had a steady inflation, but it has been much more severe in the latter country. Brazil's inflation seemed to level off in 1957, but 1958 again saw an upsurge in prices (Table 12).

No single cause can be pinpointed for the inflation in Latin America. In general, it reflects the pressures under which these economies have operated to develop rapidly and maintain rising living standards. The inflation has been accomplished by an expansion of bank credit, not only to finance private investment, but also to cover budgetary deficits and international borrowing to cover balance of payments deficits. In many instances, once started, the inflation has fed on itself. Price increases have been followed by wage increases which in turn necessitated a further rise in prices, and so on.

In 1959 Argentina undertook an austerity program to halt the inflation and many countries have instituted policy reforms which they hoped would curb price increases. In general, there has not yet been the kind of harsh action necessary to contain the inflation. The most serious consequence, already mentioned, is the discouragement to savings. In addition, there is a general debilitating effect on the price system through the distortion of prices resulting from an uneven upward movement. Both domestic and international indebtedness also exercise an adverse influence on economic growth and are a constant source of further inflation, as well as instability.

*Foreign Trade.* While world trade has been climbing consistently each year, the trade of Latin America has been characterized in the postwar period by a series of fits and starts, with a generally upward trend. In 1957 Latin American exports reached an all time high of $8.5 billion, followed by a decline in 1958. Exports in 1954 to 1955 and again in 1956 to 1957 displayed relatively little change, although exports increased during 1956 by more than 7%. If Venezuela, the only country which each year since 1953 has had an increasing volume, as well as value, of trade, is eliminated from the series, then Latin America does not indicate any clear trend. Latin American trade in recent years has the following principal features: (1) slow growth, (2) instability in volume and prices, and (3) continued heavy concentration in relatively few products.

The volume of exports of each Latin American country has displayed erratic movements since 1952. Argentina and Brazil had an increasing volume between 1952 and 1954, a break in 1954, and then an upward trend between 1955 and 1957. Chile has had an increasing volume since 1953 and Colombia has had a decreasing volume, while Bolivia's exports have remained fairly stable, but below the 1953

### Table 13

### Volume of Exports of Latin American Countries

### (1953 = 100)

|  | 1952 | 1954 | 1955 | 1956 | 1957 | 1958 |
|---|---|---|---|---|---|---|
| Latin America | 90 | 98 | 107 | 116 | 118 | -- |
| Argentina | 54 | 108 | 94 | 103 | 111 | 106c |
| Bolivia | 99 | 87 | 89 | 86 | 87 | 68d |
| Brazil | 89 | 114 | 111 | 115 | 107 | 112b |
| Chile* | 120 | 119 | 131 | 143 | 154 | -- |
| Colombia | 79 | 88 | 87 | 78 | 75 | 87f |
| Costa Rica | 97 | 94 | 98 | 73 | 96 | 74c |
| Cuba | 88 | 84 | 92 | 106 | 104 | -- |
| Dominican Republic | 104 | 98 | 106 | 117 | 117 | 50c |
| Ecuador** | 106 | 121 | 151 | 142 | 165 | 183f |
| El Salvador | 100 | 94 | 112 | 115 | 139 | 141a |
| Guatemala | 94 | 94 | 98 | 107 | 100 | -- |
| Haiti | 124 | 112 | 108 | 117 | -- | -- |
| Honduras | 94 | 75 | 71 | 98 | 93 | 66b |
| Mexico*** | 98 | 111 | 150 | 180 | 121 | 191d |
| Nicaragua | 96 | 113 | 158 | 122 | 140 | 101e |
| Panama | 94 | 116 | 138 | 120 | 143 | 109f |
| Paraguay | 89 | 93 | 94 | 122 | 105 | 173e |
| Peru | 93 | 103 | 111 | 123 | 116 | 160c |
| Uruguay | 74 | 92 | 73 | 92 | 54 | 62c |
| Venezuela**** | 103 | 108 | 122 | 139 | 155 | 148e |

*Copper                              a June
**Bananas                            b August
***Cotton                            c September
****Petroleum                        d October
                                     e November
                                     f December

Source:  International Financial Statistics, March, 1959; United Nations, Monthly Bulletin of Statistics, February, 1959.

level. The Central American states have generally exported an increasing volume. Uruguay's exports have been low relative to 1953, the best year in the last six years. In 1957 exports were only slightly more than one-half of the 1953 level (Table 13).

The volume exported reflects, of course, all of the supply and demand conditions of the products involved in the trade, as well as the characteristics of the product mix. In Latin America the nature of the exports in many cases dictates the volume exported. Food, beverages, textiles, and other products primarily for consumer use are particularly sensitive to demand and price conditions. Latin American exports are dominated by such products.

Heavy dependence upon a relatively few primary products (and most of them for consumers) is a major characteristic of the exports of each Latin American country. Indeed, primary products often dominate the entire economy of a given country. Expansion of non-export and non-primary product sectors has taken place, frequently at a faster pace, but the dependence of these countries has not declined significantly in the postwar years.

Diversification has become increasingly a problem, since, as Latin American economies have grown, their import demands have also grown. In order to maintain exports, however, these countries have been forced into expanding the primary product export sectors, the dependence on which has had such a debilitating short-run effect on the economies through price and volume fluctuations. Import substitute sectors have not kept pace with the increases in demand for imported products and new export goods have been limited in number and relatively slow growing.

*Reliance on Primary Products.* For Latin America as a whole, the fifteen most important commodity exports have provided 70% to 90% of the export earnings in the postwar period and the five most important have earned between 60% and 70% of the total. The extent to which Latin American exports are concentrated in a few primary products is demonstrated by the fact that in every country except Mexico and Peru exports of three primary products account for more than 50% of the country's total exports. Peru's proportion reaches 50% if four products are included and Mexico if five products are included. In many instances the first three products earn 80% to 90% of the foreign exchange.

In 15 countries, a single product accounted for one-half or more of exports in 1957: Bolivia, tin, 60%; Brazil, coffee, 61%; Chile, copper,

67%; Colombia, coffee, 75%; Costa Rica, coffee, 59% (first half 1958);
Cuba, sugar, 81%; Dominican Republic, sugar, 55%; Ecuador, bananas,
52%; El Salvador, coffee, 79%; Guatemala, coffee, 72%; Haiti, coffee,
71%; Honduras, bananas, 60%; Panama, bananas, 71%; Uruguay,
wool, 50%; and Venezuela, petroleum, 92%. In the five remaining
countries, coffee is 44% of Nicaragua's exports; cotton is 23% of
Mexico's exports and 21% of Peru's exports; in Paraguay, timber
constitutes 29% of total exports; in Argentina, meat is 28% of total
exports. In 1957 five products constituted more than 60% of total
exports for all of Latin America. As yet there is no perceptible trend
indicating a loosening of the grip of these products on the trade and
economies of Latin America (Table 14).

There is, of course, nothing wrong *per se* with specialization, perhaps
even to the extent to which it is practiced by Latin America. The
unhealthy result arises from the combination of supply and demand
factors, which for many of these products, may lead to a serious
imbalance in the Latin American economies because of the vulnerability of export products. Many of these exports are crop
products. So far as any given market period is concerned, the supply
in that market is relatively inelastic, perhaps even fixed. Further,
many of the products, particularly those which are destined for
consumers, tend also to have a relatively inelastic demand. Thus,
either a shift in supply or demand will tend to have a greater than
proportionate impact upon price. For instance, suppose that the
demand shifts, so that buyers of any given product are willing to
purchase more of the product at every price. With supply fixed, the
price rises sharply. Certainly, Latin American countries have no
objection to this—a circumstance which has been happening over
a long period of time as Latin American markets, with growing
incomes, want to drink more coffee, eat more meat and bananas, and
use more textiles.

Unfortunately, however, the problem does not end there. There
is also the reverse result. Suppose, because of the competition of
African coffees, European markets decide they will buy less coffee
from Brazil at every price level. With a fixed supply, the price falls
precipitously. In recent years these two phenomena have happened
to a disconcerting degree. When inelastic demand, coupled with
inelastic supply, has resulted in an unusually high price, the new high
price encourages producers and impels countries to stimulate the
production and marketing of even more of the item in the next and

## Table 14

### Structure of Latin American Exports in 1957

| Country | Products | Per cent |
|---|---|---|
| Latin America | Coffee,[2] petroleum,[2] sugar, wool, cotton | 61 |
| Argentina | Wheat,[1] corn, meat,[2] wool,[1] hides, linseed, quebracho extract | 71 |
| Bolivia | Tin,[6] tungsten, lead, zinc, silver | 87 |
| Brazil | Coffee,[6] cotton, cacao | 69 |
| Chile | Copper,[6] nitrates[1] | 77 |
| Colombia | Coffee,[7] petroleum[1] | 89 |
| Costa Rica | Bananas,[3] coffee,[4] cacao | 93 |
| Cuba | Sugar,[8] tobacco | 87 |
| Dominican Republic | Sugar,[5] coffee,[1] cacao,[1] tobacco | 86 |
| Ecuador | Bananas,[5] coffee,[2] cacao,[1] rice | 92 |
| El Salvador | Coffee,[7] cotton[1] | 90 |
| Guatemala | Coffee,[7] bananas[1] | 85 |
| Haiti | Coffee,[6] sisal,[1] sugar | 91 |
| Honduras | Bananas,[5] coffee,[1] silver, wool[1] | 85 |
| Mexico | Cotton,[2] coffee,[1] lead, copper, zinc | 54 |
| Nicaragua | Coffee,[4] cotton,[3] sesame | 81 |
| Panama | Bananas,[7] cacao | 74 |
| Paraguay | Timber,[2] cotton,[1] quebracho, hides | 62 |
| Peru | Cotton,[2] sugar,[1] lead,[1] petroleum, copper, silver, zinc | 67 |
| Uruguay | Wool,[5] meat,[2] hides, wheat, linseed oil | 90 |
| Venezuela | Petroleum[9] | 92 |

| | | |
|---|---|---|
| 1 -- 10-19 per cent | 4 -- 40-49 per cent | 7 -- 70-79 per cent |
| 2 -- 20-29 per cent | 5 -- 50-59 per cent | 8 -- 80-89 per cent |
| 3 -- 30-39 per cent | 6 -- 60-69 per cent | 9 -- 90-100 per cent |

Source: <u>International Financial Statistics</u>, February, 1959.

succeeding market periods. This, however, results in a shift in the supply relationship, so that in the next market period there is a sharp decline in the price.

*Stocks.* Countries have attempted to hold back the product, creating an artificial supply condition, in an effort to prevent price declines. The result is an accumulation of stocks, which in part does help to keep the price up, but which also acts as a general depressant on prices, since producer and consumer alike know of the existence of the stocks and the possibility that a country in desperation may use the stocks, thus breaking the price. Large stocks also tie up a considerable amount of capital, preventing its useful employment for development purposes. Since there are several producing countries for many of the products, even in Latin America, price maintenance is difficult and risky. Even large-scale and well-financed stabilization schemes break down.

Even so, Latin American countries are members of stabilization programs. Bolivia, for example, is a member of the International Tin Council. Latin American coffee producers entered into an agreement in September, 1958, to withhold coffee from the market and to sell in the market in accordance with pre-determined shares. It remains to be seen how effectively the price is stabilized and whether or not stocks can be reduced. African producers, who are becoming an increasing element in world coffee production, are not parties to the agreement and could interfere with its operation, especially in the European markets. Furthermore, the existing large stocks hanging over the market may tend to be a destabilizing factor and the agreement has not removed the incentive for greater production—the artificially high price, which may result in still further accumulation of stocks. Recently the supply has been growing at about 5% per year; demand has been growing at only about 3% per year. Only lower prices and a cut-back in production will permit stabilization in the coffee market.

The most apparent consequence of heavy concentration on a relatively few products is the instability of prices for Latin American products. High prices predominated during the Korean war period, but since 1954 Latin America's export prices have been falling. With 1953 as 100, the export price index for the area was 109 in 1954, declined to about 101 in 1955-1957, and stood at 94 in November, 1958. Some countries have been noticeably harder hit. At the end of the third quarter, 1958, Argentina's export proceeds were less than three-fourths those earned in 1953. Brazil was in about the same condition.

At the end of the third quarter, 1958, Uruguay's export price index was 69, compared to 100 in 1953. Nearly every country experienced some decline, relative not only to 1953, but also in relation to 1956, and the trend accelerated in late 1957 and 1958. An examination of the trends in export prices of particular primary products shows the same decline. About the only major products whose prices

Table 15

Latin American Export Price Indices

(1953 = 100)

| | 1952 | 1954 | 1955 | 1956 | 1957 | 1958 |
|---|---|---|---|---|---|---|
| Bananas* | 99 | 100 | 101 | 102 | 106 | 112d |
| Beef - Argentina | 80 | 101 | 95 | 75 | 72 | 90d |
| Cacao - Brazil | 102 | 162 | 108 | 77 | 92 | 142c |
| Coffee* | 93 | 134 | 98 | 100 | 98 | 74e |
| Copper** | 104 | 99 | 141 | 128 | 86 | 89e |
| Cotton - Mexico | 107 | 108 | 99 | 95 | 92 | 73c |
| Hides - Argentina | 106 | 87 | 67 | 63 | 52 | 60d |
| Lead** | 145 | 105 | 115 | 126 | 103 | 79e |
| Petroleum - Venezuela | 98 | 108 | 108 | 105 | 103 | 106a |
| Sugar - Cuba | 109 | 96 | 93 | 98 | 120 | 105e |
| Tin - Bolivia | 127 | 100 | 98 | 106 | 99 | 97c |
| Wheat - Argentina | 98 | 72 | 71 | 64 | 62 | 58d |
| Wool - Uruguay | 94 | 105 | 90 | 84 | 95 | 64b |
| Zinc - Mexico | 143 | 88 | 96 | 113 | 113 | 71b |

*U.S. import price            a August            d November
**U.K. import price           b September         e December
                              c October

Source: International Financial Statistics, March, 1959.

increased were cacao beans, sugar, and petroleum. The general reason for the price declines has been the growing supply capabilities of Latin American, as well as competing primary producers, in the face of a stable or slow growing demand. In 1957 and 1958 the recession in the United States had an adverse effect upon the prices of some products (Table 15).

While export prices were universally declining, Latin American import prices have been increasing, thus worsening the area's terms of trade even more. With 1953 as the base, import prices increased to 104 in 1956, 107 in 1957, and in September, 1958, stood at 106. Thus, Latin American terms of trade, which improved from 100 in 1953 to 110 in 1954, have deteriorated steadily since that time, to 101 in 1955, 98 in 1956, 94 in 1957, and 88 in September, 1958.

*Prospects for Latin America.* The economic and trading position of Latin America, never secure, has deteriorated seriously since 1958 and in 1959 is in a perilous condition. While progress has been made, it has not been sufficient to rate the area as fast-growing. Inflation continues to plague many of the economies and the export sectors exercise unusually great influence throughout the economies.

The short-term outlook, furthermore, is not good. Stocks of some products, notably coffee, continue to accumulate and despite the new agreement, the prospects for price increases are slim. Higher production levels of many primary products may well be sufficient to keep prices low or depress them even further. Import demands, on the other hand, remain high, not only for capital goods for developmental purposes, but also for essential current imports. Everywhere in Latin America, balances of payments are under strong pressure and short-term borrowing to meet immediate trade balances is growing.

The International Monetary Fund, the Export-Import Bank, the United States Government Development Loan Fund, the International Bank for Reconstruction and Development and many other agencies, in cooperation with the governments of Latin American countries, are attempting to correct not only the temporary problems, but also the fundamental structural imbalances through loans, grants, and technical assistance. Regional cooperation is increasing and serious consideration is being given to the establishment of a regional common market. In April, 1959, the charter for an inter-American development bank was drawn up, with every indication of whole-hearted hemispheric support.

On the Latin American side, there is increasing evidence that these countries are prepared to undertake major economic reforms to improve the efficiency of their industries and the operations of their economies. Many countries are also becoming more receptive to private foreign investment as a supplement to their own resources and to conserve foreign exchange. Some countries, notably Argentina, are taking stringent steps to curb inflation. Latin America appears ready to cooperate in regional and international organizations on matters of trade liberalization, promotion of exports, and price stabilization.

*       *       *

The fundamental economic problems of Latin America should not be under-estimated. While some countries in the area have the resource base for substantial economic development, it will be a long and tortuous process with no guarantee of success. The present situation may well be worse than usual, but it is possible that even with gradually rising per capita income, more diversification, and less reliance on unstable trade the Latin American economies may fall behind the industrialized countries in relative rates of growth. Even so, the countries of Latin America and the world seem prepared to make an effort to take advantage of the economic development potential that does exist in Latin America.

Given the economic position of Latin America, it is not difficult to understand why these countries have not always rebuffed the overtures of the Soviet-East European area and in some instances have even encouraged more extensive trade and economic relations.  Probably more than anything except their freedom as democratic states, the countries of Latin America want and need economic and industrial development.  It is in the light of these basic goals that Latin Americans judge the economic activities of the Soviet Union and Eastern Europe in their countries.  If trade and credit are not thought by the Latin Americans to threaten or prejudice their political freedom and flexibility of actions, while providing either capital goods for industrial development or imports on current account without the use of dollars or sterling, then they tend to be welcomed.[1]

In addition, insofar as the Soviet Union and Eastern Europe represent new customers, then Latin American countries feel that they will be able to pay for their own development programs.  Even so, Latin American countries set a higher value on political and economic freedom than on economic development, so that a skeptical attitude toward sources of supply representing alien ideologies remains and the area can be expected to anticipate and resist any economic and political pressure.

The motives and objectives of Latin America in its dealings with the Soviet-East European bloc are predominantly economic in nature and derive from the particular economic problems of each country.  In order to develop the full scope of Latin American objectives, an analysis of the details of hundreds of specific circumstances for each country would be required.  There are, however, at least six motives which are common to all countries.  They are:   (1) to find new customers for exports, (2) to acquire imports from new sources of supply, (3) to conserve foreign exchange, particularly dollars and sterling, (4) to maintain export prices, by expanding their market and trading on a bilateral basis, (5) to help keep import prices down, by developing new suppliers and encouraging competition among suppliers, and (6) to obtain credit on favorable terms.

In nearly all transactions one or more of these objectives are apparent.  In October, 1958, Mr. Jose V. Liceaga, member of the

Argentinian Parliament and chief negotiator on the $100 million Soviet oil equipment line of credit, is reported to have said: "The terms are most favorable. . . . Repayment will be made in wool, hides, quebracho extract and other traditional export items over a period of seven years. This will make it unnecessary for us to draw on our foreign exchange reserves, which are needed for expansion in other branches of the economy. . . . We have the deposits, the workers, and the technicians, but not enough modern equipment. That is why the present agreement is so important for us. . . . It demonstrates that there are wide opportunities for acquiring Soviet capital goods in exchange for traditional export commodities. The agreement may stimulate broader trade between the U.S.S.R. and Latin America on a mutually beneficial basis."[2] This quotation touches upon Soviet and East European motives and capabilities, which are discussed at length in Chapters VII and VIII.

*Political Motives.* Political objectives in Latin American trade with the Soviet-East European bloc are not wholly absent, however. There are at least three important and pervasive non-economic considerations in this trade. Latin America is aware that the United States is conscious of expanding economic contacts between its neighbors and the Soviet Union and Eastern Europe. Latin America is also aware that the United States is not particularly pleased by these developments because of the possible implications of the trade.

Latin American countries have not shied away from publicity about Soviet and East European offers of trade and credit, partly because of the hope that the United States will be more sympathetic. Indeed, there has been a tendency to call attention to each transaction. This has not been done with the specific hope or expectation that the United States would feel compelled to follow suit, but with the rather general anticipation that if the United States is fully conscious of the details of the transactions and the fact that Latin American countries feel it necessary to consider seriously such economic relations, then the United States will tend to take the area's problems more seriously and will try to be as helpful as possible.

Furthermore, when a country is harmed by Soviet and East European activities, as Bolivia was recently, the United States gets appeals on the grounds that a single little country "cannot fight Russian imperialism alone," as a full-page advertisement, paid for by Bolivia, in a leading newspaper in the United States announced in 1958.[3] These are traditional devices in a bipolar world. They are gentle reminders to public leaders and public opinion in the United States that Latin America is important. Certainly the moves of Latin America in this respect do not begin to approach the international blackmail which was attempted by Egypt in 1956 when its officials indicated that the West was bidding against the Soviet Union for the building of the Aswan High Dam. When the Western offers were withdrawn, the supposed Soviet offers were disclosed as a myth. The High Dam has still not been started, although in the fall of 1958 the Soviet Union agreed to provide about one-fourth of the Dam's foreign exchange requirements.[4]

There is a negative aspect, however, to this potential political motive. Generally speaking, the countries of Latin America are not particularly anxious to jeopardize their existing good relations with the United States and European powers. If doing business with the Soviet Union and Eastern Europe is felt to have such an unfavorable impact that either the governments or investors in Western countries might be alienated, without offsetting benefits from trade with the bloc, then some Latin American countries might be quite reluctant to enter negotiations for substantial trade with the Soviet-East European bloc.

More important, however, than the disfavor which Latin Americans might engender in the United States and Europe is their own reluctance to do business with the Soviet Union and Eastern Europe. This reluctance is based partly upon Soviet and East European commercial policy, which as had been noted, is far from satisfactory. Furthermore, because of their heritage of freedom, their intense individualism, and their adherence to the Roman Catholic Church, Latin Americans tend to look with disfavor on regimes which espouse the Communist philosophy. The indigenous Communist parties are both a help and a hindrance to expanded trade. They are moderately effective propaganda agents for the Soviet Union, but as political parties and a potential source of subversion, these parties have earned the displeasure of most of the regimes of Latin America. Anything which even remotely resembles helping local Communists, or the countries about which they incessantly talk, is anathema to the Latin American governments and trading circles. Thus, before trade can take place, significant political and ideological hurdles must be cleared.[5]

*Economic Motives.* These motives and restraints exercise some influence, but when countries are desperate for economic succor, as many Latin American countries have been, economic considerations tend to override the arguments for or against economic relations either on non-economic grounds or based upon past performance. An almost universal quotation can be attributed to the trade ministers not only of Latin American countries, but of all primary producing countries: "We have a product to sell. We must sell it if we are to survive. We will sell it to any country that will buy it."[6] On purely economic grounds such sentiments have merit, but clearly ignore the use of trade as a political weapon.

*"Surplus" Problem.* The basic economic motivation of Latin America centers about a "surplus" of primary products, at existing price levels, and an insatiable desire for capital goods and other imports. During the 1950's it was relatively easy for Latin American countries to produce beyond the world demand for their products. The high prices of the early 1950's, partly a result of the Korean war, made it attractive to expand production with the expectation that the demand would be maintained. When the Korean war halted, however, demand dropped off. Yet supply continued to increase, putting pressure on prices and making it mandatory that new customers be found.

It is as a new customer that Latin America tends to view the Soviet Union and Eastern Europe. Some political, financial, and trading officials in Latin American countries have observed the burgeoning population, particularly of the Soviet Union, the demonstrable industrial progress of the Soviet economy, and the gradually rising standard of living. Under these circumstances some Latin Americans believe that it is only natural for the Soviet Union and Eastern Europe to be looking for new sources of supply for food and raw materials and a market for industrial goods. And Latin America, they argue, is the ideal place for the Soviet area to satisfy its needs.

Proponents of this trade frequently point to the stagnant livestock population of the Soviet Union and low per capita meat consumption, for Argentina's benefit; to the Soviet need for wool with which to clothe its growing population, for Uruguay's benefit; to Soviet high-cost copper and other minerals needed for the expansion of industry, for the benefit of Chile and other countries; to a population just now learning the joys of drinking coffee, for the benefit of Brazil, Colombia, and a host of other countries; and to the growing Soviet capability to export capital goods, for the benefit of every Latin American country.

The argument applies with even greater force for Eastern Europe with whom many Latin American countries have had trade experience and whose economic position seems even better suited for Latin America's purposes than that of the Soviet Union.

*Capital Goods Source.* Those who favor trade with the Soviet Union and Eastern Europe also argue that these countries are a vast store-house of capital goods and other products needed for Latin American economic development. The same growth that makes the Soviet-East European area such a profitable market, according to this view, also makes it a source of supply for capital goods and other materials. To Argentina and Brazil, who spend a large portion of their scarce foreign exchange earnings on oil, it is both a source of oil for current needs from the expanding Volga and Rumanian fields and the promise of oil equipment to develop their own oil resources. In Uruguay oil is also a primary need. For Chile and Bolivia the Soviet Union and Eastern Europe are regarded by some as a supplier of mining equipment, and all countries look hopefully for capital equipment.

Almost as important as the trade offers, however, is the technique which circumvents the foreign exchange markets. Under bilateralism, Latin American countries are led to believe that they do not need dollars or sterling or gold. The Latin American country deposits its own money in a special clearing account when imports are paid for and the Soviet Union or an East European country deposits its own money in a similar account when paying for its Latin American imports. Trade, regulated by the agreement and carefully supervised, balances exactly and there is no use of foreign exchange. If trade for any reason does not balance, then the country with the export surplus cuts down deliveries and increases its imports and the other country does just the reverse. The fact that bilateral agreements have not worked out according to theory has dulled but not fully extinguished the Latin American persuasion that bilateral trade agreements are a useful technique.

Some Latin Americans believe that three of the principal goals of Latin American countries are achieved in trade with the Soviet Union and Eastern Europe. They have ostensibly found a new market and disposed of their products in that market. They have found a new supplier and acquired needed imports from that supplier, all without the use of any foreign exchange. There can be no doubt that superficially the entire package is a very attractive one to Latin American countries, one not easily turned down.

Latin America is also interested in improving its terms of trade. It is well known that the Soviet Union and Eastern Europe have no independent foreign pricing system. In each country, an internal price system is used, in part, to allocate resources in accordance with the planners' desires, but these prices are unrelated to world prices. There is no convertibility into world currencies for any of the countries, nor even any intra-bloc transferability. The trade of the Soviet Union and Eastern Europe purports to be at world market prices. As has been demonstrated earlier, however, this practice often results in a deterioration in the terms of trade for Latin America even while appearing to improve them.

*Attraction of Trade.* The appeal of trading at world market prices and the possibility of improving Latin American terms of trade, however, cannot be denied. Assuming that other aspects of Soviet and East European commercial policy are comparable to those of other countries, selling to the Soviet Union at the world market price as opposed to either selling at a lower price to another country or not selling at all is an attractive prospect. Furthermore, buying capital equipment at world market prices with clearing account dollars when the alternative is capital equipment, perhaps even of a somewhat superior quality, with scarce or non-existent foreign exchange, is also regarded as highly desirable by some Latin American countries.

The key question, which cannot be fully answered in the abstract, is whether or not terms of trade are actually improved. The answer depends upon all of the characteristics of Soviet and East European commercial policy and upon the supply and demand elasticities of the products imported and exported. In the simplified abstract case which is presented to Latin Americans by the Soviet Union, the appearance is given that bilateral trade at world market prices definitely improves their terms of trade. It is frequently this appearance, rather than the realities, which influences these countries to trade.

For many years most Latin American countries have been in debt to major world powers and international institutions. Despite the debt burden, there seems to be no limit to the Latin American need for credit. The posture of the Soviet Union and Eastern Europe since 1953 has encouraged some Latin American countries to believe that this area is a source of substantial amounts of credit for economic development. Indeed, in isolated instances, Soviet area countries have made modest loans to Latin American countries. The Soviet Union and Eastern Europe have made, moreover, substantial loan offers and on apparently favorable terms—7 to 12 years repayment period and a "political" interest rate of $2\frac{1}{2}\%$.

To all outward appearances, Latin America's motives and goals for trade meet a favorable response with the Soviet Union and Eastern Europe. Considered in the abstract, what the Soviet Union and Eastern Europe propose is ideal, as it is intended to be: expanded Latin American exports and imports without the use of foreign exchange, improvement in Latin American terms of trade with mutually beneficial exchange, and credit on favorable terms. The limited experience of Latin America in trade with the Soviet Union and Eastern Europe does not provide a basis for these countries to make a completely realistic judgment, so that many of the trade decisions must necessarily be founded upon as yet incompletely substantiated promises about the Soviet and East European conduct of trade.

\*　　\*　　\*

Just as economic planning, but not necessarily after the Soviet model, impresses many Latin Americans as the most satisfactory method of economic organization for the future, so trade with the Soviet Union and Eastern Europe, the countries which proved that planning can work, strikes some as the trading area of the future. Soviet propagandists, including the highest officials, have spread a wide network of half-truths and misleading statements about the rate of Soviet growth, about Soviet industry and living standards, and about the conduct of Soviet trade. Latin Americans, having had little contact or interest in the Soviet Union until the past few years, have no adequate way to defend themselves against these gross exaggerations. There can be little doubt that some of the Latin American motivation for trade is based upon a partially incorrect and certainly incomplete knowledge of the potential trading partners.

## VII SOVIET AND EAST EUROPEAN CAPABILITIES, PRIORITIES, AND GROWTH

The impact of the Soviet Union and Eastern Europe upon Latin America through trade and other economic relations has not been completely favorable because of the former's commercial policy and trade performance. This direct method of gaining influence is, however, only one way of indicating and measuring the impact. Of equal significance in influencing Latin American as well as other countries has been an indirect approach—through example. The Soviet Union has taken great pains to broadcast widely claims about the size, capabilities, and growth of its economy and the advantages of the social, economic, and political system on which it is based.

The indirect method has been very successful in Latin America, where there exists only a limited knowledge of the Soviet and East European economies. Observable events, such as the Soviet earth satellites and lunar probes, have added to the impact. The point has now been reached where Latin America has, in many instances, a grossly inflated and distorted view of the Soviet economy, a view only slightly discounted from that which the Soviet Union reports officially for world consumption.

That there are significant — and highly distinctive — departures between reality and the Soviet official line on its economy has been manifest since the beginning of the Communist regime. Students of Soviet affairs have noted an increasing gap between the facts and what the Soviet Union has reported. The discrepancy is based partly on the fact that the Soviet economy is in fact growing and now possesses greater capabilities than in the past, and hence there is now more to point to with pride, and partly on a few spectacular technical achievements which seem to make the Soviet official line more credible. It should be made clear that outside scholars have seldom accused the Soviet Union of telling falsehoods, but it is also seldom that scholars have accused the Soviet Union of telling the complete, undistorted truth.

It is clearly not possible in a few pages to survey the entire Soviet and East European economies. Such evaluations have been done elsewhere in a competent fashion.[1] It is of some significance, however, that the principal elements in the force of the Soviet example be analyzed to indicate just what is the carrier of influence to Latin

America. No attempt will be made to discuss the social and political elements of the Soviet regime. First and foremost, Latin Americans are impressed by the growth of the Soviet economy, particularly its industrial growth. Related to this are the present size and capabilities of the economy, as well as the Soviet trading position.

*Size.* The Soviet Union produced in 1958 a gross national product of about $150 billion.[2] This implies an economy approximately one-third the size of the United States and if about $50 billion is added for Eastern Europe then about 45% that of the United States. Size in itself, however, says very little. The Soviet Union claims that its industrial production, as a proportion of total product, is greater than in the United States, but there is reason to doubt this, despite the disproportionate emphasis given to heavy industry in the Soviet Union. The claims of the Soviet Union are based upon statistics and statistical procedures which are a state secret. It is also certain that Soviet agriculture requires proportionately larger resources, notably of manpower, than its counterpart in the United States. Soviet agriculture employs nearly one-half of the total labor force.

Despite a somewhat distorted economic structure, the Soviet economy has now reached the point where it must be reckoned as fully capable of undertaking substantial measures for the welfare of its people, for its continued growth, both in industry and agriculture, and for the maintenance of its military prowess. In essence, the Soviet Union can do anything within reason that it wants to do, but it cannot do everything simultaneously. As in even the most affluent economy, a strict priority schedule must be followed. In most economies these priorities are determined by private independent decision-making units. In the Soviet Union, Eastern Europe, mainland China, and to a lesser extent in some other economies, a highly centralized and detailed economic plan, determined by the political leadership and implemented by a professional class of planners, is imposed on production units and consumers.

Having divorced the allocation of resources from supply and demand considerations, including pressure from consumers, the political leadership and the bureaucracy distribute the product in accordance with their own conception of the national welfare. For the Soviet Union and Eastern Europe, the leadership has determined that the national welfare is best served by giving the highest priority to economic growth, particularly in industry. This is tempered by the desire of the Soviet Union to maintain a strong military establishment and to provide consumers with a gradually rising standard of living. The result has been depressed living conditions in the Soviet Union, below those of its East European dependents, and far below those of Western Europe and the United States.

*Economic Growth.* In explaining Soviet economic growth, it must be remembered that Russia would have grown under any regime. Indeed, Tsarist Russia made substantial progress with considerable assistance from private foreign capital and during the last quarter of the 19th century industrial growth in Russia was not significantly below the present rates of Soviet industrial growth. Russia has the natural resources, manpower, geographic and climatic conditions, and enterprise to be a great power under a democratic regime, under Communism, or under any kind of economic, social, and political system.

The distinctive Communist contribution was and is the decision, taken early in the regime, to concentrate on building national power, through the erection of an industrial state. Thus, the product-mix under Communism is different from that which would have been developed under another system. It cannot be argued, however, that Russian growth at present is greater because of Communism. In addition to the decision to maximize growth, Communism imposed a planning organization which does everything except provide incentives, imposed upon agriculture the amazingly destructive collective farm organization, abolished all methods for determining objectively the priority schedule, built up an incredibly top heavy bureaucracy, and developed a social and political system unsympathetic toward individualism, as well as individual ambition and growth.

The Soviet Union chose growth as the means to its ends for a variety of complex reasons. Perhaps the most important reason was an obsessive fear of the capitalist countries which displayed some enmity toward the early Communist regime. To the Communists the obvious solution was to rival and surpass the industrial powers which they regarded as antagonists and a threat to their existence.

Despite its growth, however, this fear from its early days has never been allayed. Indeed, the Soviet Union purports now to have even greater fear because of what it regards as jealousy on the part of the Western powers. Related, of course, to these antagonisms, are the power-seeking characteristics of the Soviet leadership and the conviction that the Soviet Union is the bulwark and protector of Communism everywhere and will eventually lead a Communist world. Strong nationalism also assists in explaining Soviet economic growth. Russia is a proud, virile, and intensely patriotic nation, sharing many of the drives and ambitions of the other European countries. Underlying all of these reasons is the Communist ideology which has a predisposition toward economic growth and an emphasis on materialistic and economic explanations for all historical processes.

*Estimates of Soviet Growth.* The evidence concerning Soviet economic growth is somewhat obscure. It is, of course, easy to find indices of growth. Statistics on growth from Soviet sources abound and Western scholars have devoted much effort to unravelling the meaning of Soviet figures. The fact remains, however, that conclusive information about Soviet growth is absent. The United States Department of State has estimated the growth of gross national product at 7% per year and industrial growth at 8 to 9% per year. The Soviet Union estimates its growth at a higher figure.[3]

The Seven-Year Plan provides for an annual growth rate for industry of 8.6%. The Sixth Five-Year Plan (1956-1960) which was abandoned in 1957 envisaged industrial growth at 10.5%. The official Soviet index claimed industrial growth of 13% in 1950-1955, 11% in 1956, 10% in 1957, and 9.6% in 1958. Indices for important products are likewise declining. Machine tools reportedly grew at 10.6% in 1950-1955 but only 3% in 1958; steel was reported to have grown also at 10.6% in 1950-1955, but only 7% in 1958.

It may be legitimately asked why the Soviet Union has grown as rapidly as it has. The answer is two-fold. A part of the explanation is that officially reported Soviet growth exceeds actual growth. There is an upward bias in the index. This bias derives from the use of constant prices so that the introduction of new products, necessarily at current prices, inflates the index. It is probable that there is also a computational upward bias, but since statistical procedures are not completely known the extent of the error cannot be determined. Furthermore, the processes of production, becoming more roundabout with more intermediary products, tend to impart an upward bias to the Soviet gross production index. Urbanization also contributes to overstating real production since as the new city develops, consumer products which on the farm were not counted in the index, are increasingly included. Since the statistical practices, computational procedures, and the data are not revealed the magnitude of these and other biases cannot be determined, although it is almost certain that the overstatement is substantial. In addition, in the context of attempting to make the best statistical record possible, enterprises in the Soviet Union will make an effort to arrange their own part of the plan so that the best possible statistical results will ensue.

*Reasons for Soviet Growth.* There are also real reasons why the Soviet Union has had relatively rapid economic growth. Investment has appeared to be more productive than in the older developed economies because of the relative "youth" of capital in the Soviet Union. Initial applications of capital to productive processes tend to have high productivity compared to the processes preceding the use of capital. As more and more capital is applied, however, the productivity of each additional unit declines. Thus, in the beginning of the industrialization process rapid strides can be made with massive doses of capital. This is precisely what Tsarist Russia did in the nineteenth century and also what the Soviet Union did following the Revolution and again in the reconstruction period following the Second World War.

The amounts of capital for productive purposes were substantially increased by two related factors: extremely low depreciation rates, rates so low, in fact, that they have not been adequate to replace capital and facilities now in disrepair, and neglect of adding enough capital to facilities to ensure their successful long-run operation. Not only with respect to capital facilities but also in the extraction of resources the Soviet Union has taken the low-cost, most accessible resources first. Additional capital was made available for immediate productive purposes by the neglect of some sectors of the economy, notably agriculture, transportation, and consumer goods, and social investment.

*Declining Rate of Growth.* These factors not only help to explain the rapid growth in the past, but also point to significant reductions in the rate of growth in the future. Replacement and repair are now consuming a substantial and increasing share of total investment, leaving less for growth purposes. Depreciation policy has become more rational and while there is still a tendency to emphasize the short-run and neglect the long-run considerations, more attention is being paid to building with a view to the future. In the extractive industries, as well as in agriculture, the Soviet economy is running into increasing costs as the low-cost grades vanish and more transportation and capital facilities are required to extract a given quantity of minerals. It is no longer possible to neglect transportation. Road building is essential and rail transportation needs capital.

Agriculture has received increased attention since it became obvious that Stalinist policies were having too great an adverse effect on output. Plant and equipment are needed in greater quantities to support the consumer goods sectors. For example, even the modest television industry in the Soviet Union requires plant facilities not necessary heretofore. Social investment, particularly in housing, can no longer be ignored. The appalling condition of housing in the Soviet Union has ceased to be a social problem and has emerged as a major economic problem, operating as a strong disincentive.

The declining effectiveness of capital investment is not the sole explanation for the falling growth rate. Two other problems having serious consequences are the labor position of the Soviet Union and the technical efficiency of the economy and its planning mechanism. It has long been recognized that the high degree of centralization in the ministries in Moscow was an inefficient method of organization and in 1958 the process of decentralization began, pushing the planning process down to the regional level.

Perhaps even more important is the absence of an effective price system which deprives the economy of any objective guide to decision-making. The price system which is in use is primarily an accounting system and bears little relationship either to world prices or to domestic demand and costs. Planners operate in the dark in many of their most important decisions, leading to incorrect and costly actions. Recently, there has been a revival of discussions of value theory and an interest in a pricing system which operates more effectively as a helper in making economic decisions, but it is unlikely that a really effective pricing system is compatible with centralized planning.

There are also many organizational deficiencies, revolving around the bureaucracy necessary to implement decisions and the nature of the planning process. As an example, production, planned to be smooth, is in fact cyclical with peaks immediately preceding the end of the plan accounting period—the month, the quarter, and the year, reflecting the extreme urgency, at the end of the plan period, to fulfill the plan. The ministerial organization system, still an

important form, is not efficient, resulting in costly duplication of
facilities and frequent cross-hauls.

*Labor Shortage.* Soviet industrialization was accomplished in part
by withdrawing laborers from agricultural pursuits and pressing them
into industrial production. This process has reached the point
where further withdrawals from agriculture are not possible and the
Soviet Union has resorted to reducing the size of the Red Army to
supply labor for industry. Furthermore, in late 1958, in order to
expand the labor force, Khrushchev introduced drastic educational
reforms which had the effect of reducing the amount of education for
all but a select few young people. While it hardly represents an improvement in the Soviet educational system, this program does
perform the vital function of making more labor available. The acute
condition in Soviet industry at the present time and for the next
decade is a result of the almost unbelievably high casualties during
the Second World War. The young people that should now be
entering the labor force were just not born. For a number of years
the Soviet Union will be plagued by a serious labor shortage.

Given the capital and labor problems faced by the Soviet Union,
the need for incentives, the methods of industrialization, and the
deficiencies in the system, it is mildly surprising that the country
has done as well as it has. It has paid a fearful economic, political,
and social price to move from the fifth industrial power to the second
industrial power, jumping over Great Britain, Germany, and France,
since 1913. Even so, Soviet progress has not been more impressive
than that of other countries. The United States has done just about
as well over a comparable time period. Japan and Canada have
grown as rapidly as the Soviet Union and in the post-war period
Western Germany and Austria have nearly matched Soviet growth.

When the size, priorities, capabilities, and growth are properly
interpreted, it emerges that the Soviet economy has an impressive
record and has done just about as well as the other major world
industrial powers. There is no reason to believe, however, the myths
that have sprung up surrounding the Soviet economy. Communism
has no secret for circumventing economic laws. Its progress is
essentially of the same kind and of the same general magnitude as
other economies, with the added ingredient that it was accomplished
under extremely adverse economic, political, and social conditions.

Thus, to the discerning Latin American it is quite unlikely that the Soviet and Communist models have anything to commend them.

*Soviet Prospects.* The next decade will be a difficult one for the Soviet Union. It is unlikely that there will be sufficient investment resources to fulfill its economic plans, especially considering the fact that increasing investment will be required for facilities which do not contribute directly to increased output. It is certain there will be a severe labor shortage. These two factors, coupled with increasing strains imposed by managing, through planning, an economy the size of the Soviet economy, providing incentives, and nursing along a sick agricultural sector, make it quite unlikely that the ambitious plan will be fulfilled. The Soviet Union will not be able to "overtake the United States" by 1975 in aggregate terms, much less in per capita production, and there is no chance at all that the Soviet Union will catch up with Western Europe, much less the United States in living standards.

Eastern Europe is, of course, a net addition to Soviet economic power. The process of sovietization of the area has, however, seriously unbalanced those economies. The emphasis on industry has made them dependent upon the Soviet Union for raw materials and food. Economic growth in Eastern Europe is slower than in the Soviet Union and is also declining. However, East Germany and Czechoslovakia are important manufacturing countries, and each country makes a unique contribution to the capability and potential of the Soviet economy.

Even so, no less an authority on the Soviet economy than the British economist Alec Nove recently said: "The available evidence suggests that for the next seven years at least the attention of the Soviet leaders will be devoted primarily to the fulfilment of their very ambitious plans for the economic growth of the Soviet bloc itself. In particular, the domestic investment programme of the Soviet Union, China, and the satellites is so vast as to impose a serious strain on the capacity of the capital goods industry. The underdeveloped countries need capital goods first and foremost. It will be difficult for the Soviet bloc to spare increasing quantities of these." (*The Listener,* February 19, 1959, p. 319) The extent to which the Soviet Union and Eastern Europe provide scarce capital goods to Latin America will depend upon a calculation of economic losses against potential economic gains.

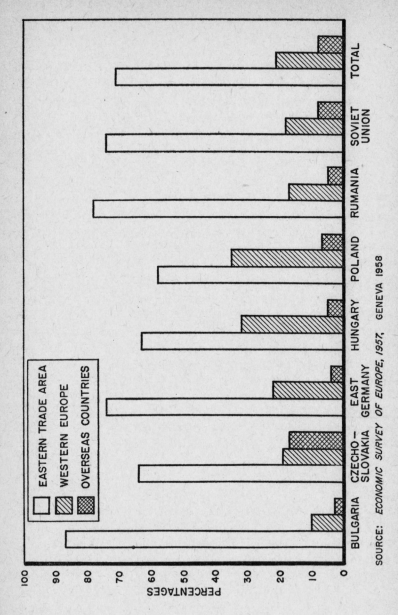

PERCENTAGES

100 90 80 70 60 50 40 30 20 10 0

EASTERN TRADE AREA

WESTERN EUROPE

OVERSEAS COUNTRIES

BULGARIA  CZECHO-  EAST  HUNGARY  POLAND  RUMANIA  SOVIET  TOTAL
SLOVAKIA  GERMANY                                  UNION

SOURCE: *ECONOMIC SURVEY OF EUROPE, 1957,* GENEVA 1958

CHART 4  SOVIET AND EAST EUROPEAN EXPORTS IN 1956

*Trade.* In international trade the Soviet Union has from the beginning of the regime followed an autarkic policy, generally characterized by an extremely low level of trade, importing only to support its industrialization program and exporting only what is necessary to pay for imports. Despite the recent increases in trade, there is no evidence that the Soviet Union will abandon autarky. Indeed, Soviet leaders have, now that Eastern Europe is secure, generalized the self-sufficiency concept to cover the entire area and three-fourths of Soviet trade is with Eastern Europe and mainland China. This policy of autarky is, however, less applicable to Eastern Europe, for whom trade is vital and whose requirements cannot be fully satisfied by the Soviet Union. Eastern Europe is also a more experienced trading area, particularly with primary producing countries. Changes in the economies of the Soviet Union and Eastern Europe indicate that trade will probably become of greater significance, but that it will continue to be modest, with however, Eastern Europe forming more stable and enduring trade ties with primary producers.

As Chart 4 indicates, the bulk of the trade of the Soviet Union and each of the East European countries is with other countries of the Soviet bloc, including China. For all these countries Western Europe as a whole is the next largest trading partner. Underdeveloped countries, only a part of the overseas trade category in the chart, constitute a very small percentage of total trade. The concentration of trade of each country with other Communist countries reflects the autarkical system which the Soviet Union maintains.

The trade of the Soviet-East European area has been increasing, particularly since 1953. Trade with underdeveloped countries has been increasing at a faster rate than with other areas, but still represents a small proportion of total trade. Soviet exports remain predominantly in primary products. Machinery and equipment exports are still a small proportion of the total. For Eastern Europe, machinery and equipment is a larger proportion of exports.

In 1958 the Soviet trade expansion came to a halt. The value of trade in 1957 and 1958 was approximately the same. The volume of Soviet trade, however, continued to increase modestly in 1958. Price declines in raw materials, which are a significant proportion of both imports and exports, are the principal explanation of the levelling off of Soviet trade. It is probable that the volume of Soviet trade will continue to grow in the future, but perhaps at a pace no faster than that of the world volume of trade.

Soviet and East European motives for international trade are a curious combination of economic and political considerations, with the emphasis on the latter in Latin America.[1]  The Soviet Union continues to pursue the dream of autarky and to some extent has generalized it to include Eastern Europe.  Yet the Soviet leaders have always realized the importance of trade as an avenue of political and economic influence and have never hesitated to use trade for political purposes.  At the same time, the Soviet Union seems to recognize the cost-reducing aspects of international trade.

Probably more than any country in the world, the Soviet Union is independent of the outside world for necessary supplies.  With the addition of Eastern Europe and mainland China, the autarkic capability of the Soviet Union is considerably enhanced.  Even so, from the very beginning of the regime, Soviet leaders sought trade, especially with Western Europe, in order to speed up industrialization with Western equipment.  The Soviet Union, despite considerable progress, is still in the industrialization process and desires capital goods, particularly precision and specialized equipment from the United States and Western Europe.[2]

As the Soviet economy has grown in its own peculiar, lopsided fashion, emphasizing industry and neglecting agriculture and extractive industries, and consumer needs, the Soviet Union has apparently found it increasingly advantageous to use its expanding industrial product export capability to import some kinds of foodstuffs, as well as partially depleted and costly minerals and metals.  Thus, economic considerations supply at least a partial underlying motive for Soviet and East European trade.

Trade with Latin America, however, shares little in this particular motivation, since there is only a limited economic basis for trade between the Soviet Union and Latin America and even Eastern Europe is only complementary in part with Latin America.[3]  In trade with some areas, such as with Latin America, and in the conduct and specific characteristics of all of its trade, the Soviet Union has fundamental political motives, with a number of specific political goals in the various regions of the world, along with its more general political aims.  Despite the possible existence of an economic motive, the basic aim of the Soviet Union is to influence the foreign and domestic policies of its trading partners.[4]

It should not be thought, however, that all Soviet aims form a straight line in the same direction. Frequently they conflict. From an economic point of view, for instance, the Soviet Union desires to realize the gains from trade, to improve its bargaining position, to assure itself of suppliers and markets, and to conserve foreign exchange. From a political point of view, the Soviet Union wishes to increase its influence, to gain world acceptance and respectability, and to have its policies, such as bilateralism, approved and accepted in the world community. Bettering its terms of trade, however, may hurt its political position. Adherence to strict bilateralism with countries who find limited import opportunities in the Soviet Union may also hurt its reputation. Frequently the Soviet Union has difficulty convincing underdeveloped countries of the sincerity of its desire to assist in their economic development. Local Communist parties, aided and abetted by the Soviet Union, often exercise a divisive influence and occasional Soviet foreign economic policies, such as underselling in some primary product markets or pressuring weaker trading partners such as Finland and Yugoslavia, tend to mar the favorable image which the Soviet Union, with other policies, has sought to create.

*Economic Motives.* In one respect, the changes in the Soviet economy over the past thirty years have resulted in a situation in which one of the fundamental economic motives and one of the fundamental political motives tend to complement each other. The sustained heavy industry investment program, the neglect of agriculture, and the increasing cost characteristics of agricultural and extractive industries are changing the relative costs of producing the different items in the Soviet Union.

With expanded plant and equipment and with greater experience in the manufacture of capital goods, the capital-building sectors have achieved economies of scale and costs of production have tended to decline. On the other hand, the extractive and agricultural sectors face a relatively more inelastic supply situation. Within limits the supply of land is fixed and raw materials sectors have expanded output by producing from less accessible land, poor and more costly deposits, and with higher transportation charges. Institutional factors, such as collectivization, have likewise retarded growth in agriculture and have increased costs.

*Changes in Relative Costs.*  In general, as the industrialization of the Soviet Union has proceeded, the costs of production of capital goods have fallen relative to the costs of production of the output of agricultural and extractive industries.  It is almost axiomatic that such a shift should take place, and it seems, based upon limited statistical evidence, that the shift had become sufficiently pronounced during the Fifth Five-Year Plan (1951-1955) that Soviet leaders began to pay more serious attention to the economic benefits of international trade.[5]  It should not be thought, however, that economic benefits are or will likely be sufficiently great that the Soviet Union will come to depend upon overseas sources of supply or that Soviet authorities will reallocate resources significantly so as to take advantage of trade.  Rather, the gains from trade will be a marginal factor, hedged in by the Soviet desire for autarky on one side and the use of trade for political purposes on the other.[6]

The Soviet Union is probably now finding that its traditional pattern of foreign trade—that is, exporting raw materials and foodstuffs and importing capital goods—is not as advantageous as it once was.  It can and does export a relatively varied line of the simpler types of capital goods, such as trucks, tractors, agricultural, construction, and mining machinery, and structural shapes.  The proportion of capital goods exports to total exports has been increasing in recent years and the proportion of grain exports has been declining.  In return, the Soviet economy is obtaining relatively greater quantities of food and industrial raw materials, as well as consumer goods, such as copper, wool, and quality foods, the domestic production of which would require a greater expenditure than is needed for the capital goods which the country exports.

The economic motive is strengthened when one considers that Eastern Europe has become a food deficit area.  In order to reorient the trade of Eastern Europe to itself, the Soviet Union has undertaken to supply many of the raw materials necessary to build an industrial base for Eastern Europe.  Thus, the expansion of trade by the Soviet Union itself, as well as by Eastern Europe and mainland China with primary producing countries may well result in a net economic gain for the Soviet Union, instead of imposing a burden.  As the Soviet-East European bloc develops its industrial capacity further, resulting in increased demands for basic resources, and as these resources are gradually depleted, it will probably become increasingly advantageous for this bloc to export more capital goods and import more raw materials. Further, as population grows, it will become more advantageous, perhaps even essential, to import greater amounts of food.

The economic motive in trade is probably strongest for the relatively more industrialized countries of Eastern Europe—Poland, Czechoslovakia, and East Germany. During the late 1940's and until about 1955, while the Soviet Union was binding their economies indissolubly to its own, these countries had no strong independent motive for trade. As the Soviet Union discovered that supplying these countries with food and raw materials placed a heavy burden on the Soviet economy, these countries gradually shifted to increasing trade outside the bloc with their former trading partners. While these countries must necessarily share Soviet political objectives, their trade is frequently a matter of vital economic necessity.[7]

*Coincidence of Motives.* Therefore, the economic motive of achieving gains from trade and the political motive of increasing Soviet-East European prestige and developing and strengthening economic and political ties with primary producing countries tend to recommend the same course of action. The underdeveloped countries of Latin America, Asia, and Africa desperately need and want capital goods for economic development in exchange for their food products and raw materials. Increasingly, the Soviet Union and Eastern Europe seem to be moving into a position to buy these products advantageously and have the capability to supply at least some of the needs of primary producing countries. Russia gains politically and economically.

The economic position of Latin America only partly fits this pattern, however. The Soviet Union and Eastern Europe have been active in trying to sell small amounts of machinery and equipment in return for some primary products. Complete complementarity, however, does not exist, in that Latin America has some raw material deficits, particularly in mineral fuels, in addition to its need for capital goods, and most Latin American countries can provide primary products of only marginal usefulness to the Soviet-East European bloc. Hence, in Latin America, the Soviet Union and Eastern Europe have altered the pattern somewhat, to take advantage of some Latin American raw material deficits.

The Soviet Union and Rumania ship petroleum and petroleum

products to Argentina, Brazil, and Uruguay, and Poland sells coal to some Latin American countries. These two products have a strong demand in Latin America. The Soviet Union and Eastern Europe are relatively well-endowed, and their competitive position with respect to other suppliers of petroleum and coal to Latin America is not seriously unfavorable. Thus, for a considerable portion of Soviet and East European trade with Latin America, the economic basis is not the capital goods for raw materials exchange about which so much is heard, but rather is a raw materials for raw materials exchange. Nonetheless, the Soviet Union has revealed its desire to ship capital goods. In selling oil to Argentina, the Soviet Union has also attempted to sell oil field and refinery equipment.

It is probable that economic motivation has played a minor role in Soviet-East European trade with Latin America. On the other hand, it is not wholly absent, especially when viewed from the point of view of the conduct of trade and the negotiation of particular transactions and agreements. The Soviet-East European bloc is quite evidently interested in improving its bargaining position, particularly its terms of trade, and in assuring itself of both a market and a source of supply. The commercial policies used by these countries are specifically designed to be able to extract maximum economic benefits from trading partners.

For example, in a setting of bilateralism, conducted under trade agreements with prices negotiated on both sides, the terms of trade are indeterminate. As has been shown, however, the terms of trade under circumstances in which the Soviet Union trades with primary producing countries tend to favor the former because of its superior bargaining power, its absence from the primary producing country's market, and the avoidance of competition with other capital goods suppliers. Soviet commercial policy operates for the most part in economic self-interest using all of the techniques and bargaining power available to that country. It is thus sometimes difficult for the Soviet Union to accord favorable treatment to its trading partners.

In sum, economic motivation provides the Soviet-East European bloc with the basis for a limited volume of mutually beneficial trade with Latin America while simultaneously serving the overriding political interests of the Soviet Union. On the other hand, the methods used by the bloc, the organization of trade, and the inexperience as well as the shrewdness of the Soviet Union tend to operate in the opposite direction, toward nullifying the favorable impression and growing influence among trading partners.

*Political Motives.* In most Soviet and East European trade with primary producers and certainly in connection with trade with Latin America, political considerations are predominant and always operative. Like the economic motives, they are sometimes conflicting. Trade is used to attempt to create a favorable view of the Soviet Union in the eyes of the world and simultaneously to reward its friends and punish its enemies, as well as to promote the ultimate aim of world domination.

In Latin America, where little is known about the Soviet Union, one of the principal aims has been to establish an impressive reputation for Soviet industry and to prove that the Soviet Union is a great power, worthy of respect and admiration. Related to this objective is the Soviet desire to demonstrate to Latin Americans that socialism can work, and that in a few short years the Soviet Union, initially weak and impotent, has risen to challenge the most advanced Western nation. Furthermore, the Soviet Union seeks to weaken the economic and political position of the United States as the leader of the Western Hemisphere, to break the solidarity which has generally characterized the outlook of the Latin American countries, and to undermine the Caracas declaration. The Soviet Union hopes to encourage the always incipient neutralism, to have in public office those who are favorable to the Soviet Union, and to be able to impress those who control the means of communication.

For the most part, however, Soviet political motives are highly specific and are related to a particular country at a particular time. The battle for men's minds rages continuously in every field of endeavor, but economic and trade relations provide the Soviet Union with a convenient specific setting in which to influence Latin American opinions. Particular transactions are proposed or concluded for highly specific purposes. For example, a few hours before the President of Argentina announced that a way had been found for oil development through the use of private foreign capital, the Soviet Union hastened to make Argentina a credit offer for oil equipment, primarily to take the sting out of its defeat in economic diplomacy and to salvage at least some influence over Argentinian oil development.

*Diplomatic Relations.* Perhaps the most pervasive, particular political motive is the desire for diplomatic recognition of all Communist countries by Latin American states and diplomatic representation in as many as possible. In April, 1958, there were 19 Soviet, Bulgarian, Czech, Hungarian, Polish, and Rumanian resident diplomatic missions in seven Latin American countries. Mainland China and East Germany are not recognized by any country in Latin America, although trade missions from both of these states have visited in the area. The Soviet Union itself has diplomatic representation in Argentina, Mexico, and Uruguay, the last being a legation. Czechoslovakia has legations in Argentina, Brazil, Bolivia, Mexico, and Uruguay, and has a consul-general in Colombia. Poland has legations in Argentina, Brazil (plus two consulates), and Mexico, and has a commercial delegation in Uruguay. Bulgaria, Hungary, and Rumania each have a legation in Argentina; Rumania is represented diplomatically in Uruguay, where Bulgaria and Hungary have commercial delegations. Hungary has a commercial delegation in Chile.

The Soviet-East European bloc in all of Latin America has only two embassies (both Soviet) and thirteen legations: in Argentina (5), Brazil (2), Bolivia (1), Mexico (2), and Uruguay (3). Diplomatic recognition itself is only slightly more widespread, with the Soviet Union, Poland, and Hungary having relations with several more countries. Several countries, including Bolivia, Costa Rica, Ecuador, El Salvador, and others have recognized the Soviet Union but have never exchanged missions and deny that diplomatic relations exist. In the postwar period there have been many cancellations of diplomatic relations with the Soviet Union. Brazil and Chile severed relations in October, 1947; Colombia in May, 1948, Cuba in April, 1952, Venezuela in June, 1952, and Guatemala in June, 1954. Czechoslovakia had legations in Ecuador and Peru, but they were closed in 1957, although diplomatic relations still exist.[8]

The Soviet Union and other Communist countries are obviously not satisfied with this state of affairs, especially when they note that a Communist country which is not a member of the "socialist camp" has wider diplomatic relations: Yugoslavia has embassies in Argentina, Brazil, Chile, and Mexico. At every opportunity the Soviet-East European bloc countries emphasize their desire for trade but point out the difficulty of conducting trade in the absence of regularized diplomatic relations. Maintaining that trade agreements could be concluded and trade would expand, they argue that Latin American

countries would greatly benefit if official representatives were exchanged.

Although most of their endeavors have been unsuccessful so far,
the Soviet Union and Eastern Europe have continued their efforts
and in some cases call upon their highest spokesmen to advance the
cause of diplomatic relations. Khrushchev on a number of occasions
has said that the absence of diplomatic relations has hampered the
development of economic relations between the Soviet Union and
Brazil and has coupled Soviet purchases of goods to Brazilian diplomatic recognition.[9] While such statements have not resulted in any
greater exchange of diplomatic personnel, Latin American nations
are obviously being importuned; some have seriously re-examined the
question of the extension of diplomatic recognition and exchange of
officials. The belief in some quarters persists that Latin America
can benefit by increased trade, even though purchased by a major
political concession. Brazil and Chile, who severed relations in 1947
because of Soviet interference in internal affairs, still wish to avoid
diplomatic contact, but the lure of potential trade may be weakening
their resolve.

Maintaining satisfactory diplomatic relations with Latin American
countries is a precarious business at best for the Soviet Union and
Eastern Europe. Periodically there is some flare up and a diplomatic
representative is charged by the government to which he is accredited
with some form of subversive or "undiplomatic" behavior. On April 3,
1959, Mexico expelled two Soviet diplomats, charging them with
having aided a Communist-inspired strike and a conspiracy to paralyze
the Mexican economy. Demands were made for severing relations
with the Soviet Union (*New York Times,* April 4, 1959). A few
days later Argentina asked the Soviet counselor to leave because of
his activities in connection with street riots in Buenos Aires. These
actions will probably not seriously disturb the structure of Soviet
and East European diplomatic representation in Latin America, but
are indicative of the difficulties the diplomats of these countries face
in their dual role as representatives of Communism and of their
country. Given a sufficiently serious incident of this nature, however,
one or more countries may withdraw recognition, as other countries
have in the past.

*Communism.* There is yet another pervasive political motive.
In addition to being one of the great nations of the world, the Soviet

Union is also the headquarters of a worldwide missionary movement which hopes either to convert or subvert all existing political regimes and establish a new economic and political system patterned after its own. Although ostensibly helping Latin American countries so that credit reflects upon the Soviet Union as a nation, Soviet leaders wish to see and are striving for weak and unstable regimes in Latin America as a prelude to the introduction of Communism.

The apparent paradox of Soviet economic assistance to and trade with underdeveloped countries, as opposed to the promotion of economic and political instability (a prelude to Communist revolutions), can be reconciled by an understanding of the ideological foundations of Communism. Convinced that no real progress is possible unless made under their system, the leaders of the Soviet Union apparently feel that their relatively meager assistance can actually speed up the historical process that will sweep all countries to Communism. By contributing to the development of industrialization in less advanced countries, the Soviet Union, from its own point of view, is simply facilitating the emergence of those economic conditions which increase the size of an industrial proletariat within which Communism theoretically thrives best. This development, nonetheless, is considerably short of economic stability and, in fact, promotes those circumstances that may advance a Communist revolution closer to reality. Therefore, those apparently charitable measures by Russia are in reality motivated by far different objectives.

Furthermore, it must be kept in mind that Soviet leaders make a sharp distinction between tactics and strategy. The goal of Communist world rule is a long-run strategic goal. Soviet leaders can justifiably argue that a pre-condition to Communism is the firm establishment of the Soviet Union as the promulgator of Communism. Whatever is necessary to establish the primacy of the Soviet Union as a world power, including assistance to underdeveloped countries not yet "ready" for Communism, is thus consistent with the eventual triumph of Communism.

*Local Communist Parties.* While appearing to help Latin American countries in their role as nations, the countries of the Soviet-East European bloc are busily engaged in sowing discord and discontent through local Communist parties in Latin America. Every Latin American country has a Communist party, but it is legal in only eight states—Argentina, Bolivia, Chile, Colombia, Ecuador, Mexico,

Uruguay, and Venezuela. The membership in Latin America is estimated at between 284,000 and 304,000, of which about 50,000 are in Brazil, 70,000 to 80,000 in Argentina, 80,000 in Mexico, 30,000 to 35,000 in Venezuela, and 20,000 to 25,000 in Chile.[10] The Communist vote, however, is somewhat larger and party influence is greater than their numbers indicate, since Communists are most active in labor unions and student movements and frequently control these organizations. In some cases, the Communist parties are able to exploit the political left since the latter, even though dedicated to democratic processes, espouses some policies which the Communists also propound.

The Communist parties are a divisive influence in Latin America, complicating democratic processes and behavior, making economic and political policy decisions difficult and complex, and serving as a constant source of unconstructive criticism and irritation. There can be no doubt that the Soviet Union, as a nation, has lent its support to the development and spread of Communism in Latin America. Leading Communist party members travel constantly to and from the Soviet Union and the Soviet Union has made funds and personnel available to Latin American Communist parties.

Even so, the extent of the influence of the Communist parties should not be overestimated. There is a deep antagonism between the ideology of the party and the Roman Catholic Church which remains in the ascendancy throughout Latin America. Perhaps as influential and effective in combatting Communism has been the democratic left, which exercises great political influence. The Communist parties in Latin America are primarily an irritant, but with a potential for mischief which requires constant vigilance in every country.

*Contradictions in Soviet Objectives.* An evaluation of Soviet and East European motives and goals in Latin America bears witness to their strong political character, with a secondary economic motive, and on both these counts, contradictory goals and behavior. The most significant discrepancy is between the promises and commitments of the Soviet Union and its actual performance in trade relations. The presence of both economic and political aims is not difficult to appreciate, given the nature of centralized decision-making in both economic and political matters in the Soviet Union. Less easy to understand is the reason for contradictions that are apparent in

Soviet policy. It would seem that a monolithic power such as the Soviet Union would have single-minded aims and that it could successfully pursue a single course of action toward Latin America.

The fact that the Soviet Union has conflicting aims derives from its position both as a nation and as the chief promulgator of an intensely missionary economic and political philosophy. The Soviet Union simultaneously wishes respect and position in the world as a nation and at the same time to replace all existing regimes with a system modelled after itself. Thus, the Soviet Union as a nation tends to undermine itself as a missionary and *vice versa*. There can be no real resolution of this conflict until the Soviet Union recognizes the unacceptability and inapplicability of Communism in Latin America. At present, both factors exercise some influence, although it must be admitted that in the past few years the Soviet Union as a nation has apparently received priority in Latin America and elsewhere.

All of the conflicts and contradictions in Soviet behavior must not be attributed to the fundamental split personality of the Soviet Union in the world today. Some of the answer must be sought in the different motives which the Soviet Union pursues in different parts of the world. It is just simply not possible for any country to present a completely uniform and consistent posture to all countries at all times, since many of the countries with whom the Soviet Union deals are in conflict with each other. For example, the sale of large quantities of tin and other metals may have the following simple explanation: The Soviet Union produces nearly enough tin for its own needs, but in order for mainland China to pay its debts to the Soviet Union the latter accepted large quantities of tin in payment. Since Soviet imports frequently exceed exports, foreign exchange is chronically short. Seeing an opportunity to sell the tin, in long supply, and acquire transferable currencies, the Soviet Union did so, bringing its trade more nearly into balance and avoiding further gold sales. In so doing, the Soviet Union had to incur the displeasure of Bolivia, Malaya, and other producers and risk a harmful international reaction. In other words, to please mainland China, the Soviet Union displeased other countries.

There are yet other explanations for Soviet contradictory behavior. Sometimes it is simply a matter of miscalculation of the effects of an act. More frequently, it is a matter of inexperience. The Soviet Union has not traded with Latin American countries either for very long or in any substantial volume. It is not a trade-wise nation and in its spurt of trade in the past few years, its lack of knowledge of the conduct of trade and of normal commercial policies has become painfully clear, often to the detriment of its trading partners. Frequently unintentionally, but sometimes intentionally, the Soviet Union has gouged a customer or supplier.

*Internal Restraints.* Two other motivational influences, both pertaining to the internal Soviet scene, affect its behavior. One is that the Soviet Union, operating as a state trader, has a tightly organized bureaucratic system which is responsible for the conduct of its trade. This organization, culminating in the Ministry of Foreign Trade, but operated by import and export corporations responsible to domestic sectoral ministries, has a complex system of plans which must be coordinated with plans for the domestic economy. The result is a relatively inflexible, bureaucracy-ridden system which frequently finds itself incapable of adjusting to the changes and vicissitudes which are inherent in international trade.

No matter what the political leaders or trade missions tell Latin American countries, trade still must go through the complicated machinery of the Soviet trade organization, in which there is many a slip between the cup and the lip. The high level policy spokesmen frequently make elaborate promises which they may fully intend to implement. But others do the implementing. The trade organizations are cost-conscious and it is their responsibility to see that the Soviet Union benefits and is not hurt by trade transactions. Indeed, the careers of lesser individuals in trade organizations hinge upon doing the best they can for their country and they are not particularly concerned with trying to gain diplomatic recognition in Brazil or impressing Argentina favorably. The operating people are frequently overridden by policy makers, but they are a constant drag on Soviet performance and account for much of the erratic behavior of the Soviet Union in foreign trade.

A further difficulty arises from a still unresolved policy conflict within the Soviet Union. When the new foreign economic policy of expanded economic contacts began to emerge in 1953, it was not without great misgivings on the part of many influential political leaders. Despite the victory of the proponents of change and despite the considerable success of Soviet external efforts so far, the more conservative element can still point to failures or to the absence of any clear-cut and decisive foreign economic victory and is continually suggesting withdrawal or retrenchment.

The East European trading partners of Latin America appear to be less interested in the political aspects of trade, are more experienced traders, and conduct their trade on much more of a straight commercial basis. Eastern Europe, however, under the general supervision of the Soviet Union, is obliged to follow Soviet policy whenever Soviet interests are vitally affected. In trade matters, Eastern Europe has some autonomy and tends to look upon trade as an economic matter. For example, Eastern Europe continues to trade with Israel, even though the Suez crisis disrupted Soviet-Israeli trade completely, with arbitration suits currently in process.

\*     \*     \*

It does not appear probable that there will be any significant change in Soviet motives and goals in Latin America in the near future. The economic motives for trade with Latin America will probably be strengthened somewhat, as will the political motives. The latter will assume greater importance should the use of trade achieve diplomatic recognition in one or more countries. The inexperience, miscalculations, and internal policy conflict will probably lessen over time, but as the Soviet Union and Eastern Europe become more important traders it is likely that export capabilities not only in capital goods, but in some raw materials, will rise. In some ways the area will become increasingly competitive with Latin America, thereby dampening the economic motive for trade. A fine balance of economic and political considerations, conflicting with and complementing one another, will determine the Soviet course, with there being no way of knowing in advance what the Soviet Union will do in any particular situation.

The only durable basis for stable and commercially acceptable trade between two countries or areas is a decisive complementary relationship between their production structures. Distinctly different and complementary product mixes can exist only when the resource endowment, cost relationships, and demand considerations within each area lead to a unique emphasis on techniques and products for each area. The exchange must necessarily result in an increase in the real income of both countries or trade will not long persist. This does not mean that these same countries might not compete vigorously in some commodities and trade advantageously in others. It does imply, however, that the scope for trade is a direct function of the extent of competition and complementarity between the two economies. It is always possible for a country to maintain "political" trade in which it incurs an economic loss. There are limits to such trade, however, which depend upon the magnitude of the loss, relative to the potential political gain.

It has been argued that the Soviet Union and Eastern Europe, with their emphasis on industrialization and relative neglect of agriculture and extractive industries have so changed their economies that they are increasingly complementary to the underdeveloped countries, which are capital deficient and have surpluses of primary products. Clarence B. Randall, special assistant to the President of the United States, has said: "The Soviet economy and that of the underdeveloped countries are complementary and ours (the United States) is antagonistic. The Soviets are short on food and fibers and long on capital goods. The new countries are long on foods and fibers and short on capital goods. This is a natural trading position." (*Soviet Progress versus American Enterprise*, Doubleday, 1958, p. 32.)

*Soviet-Latin American Complementarity.* Ignoring the larger issue of Soviet complementarity with primary producing countries in general—a question which is arguable in itself—it is worthwhile to examine in some detail Soviet-Latin American complementarity. The usual complementarity for primary producing countries is a capital goods exchange for raw materials and foodstuffs. For Latin America, it is necessary not only to study this postulate but also the possibility of complementarity based on an exchange of primary products for primary products.

Table 16

Latin American and Soviet Trade in Selected Products in 1957

(millions of U.S. dollars)

| Commodity | Latin American Exports | Soviet Exports | Soviet Imports |
|-----------|-----------------------|----------------|----------------|
| Bananas   | 129    | 0     | --  |
| Cacao     | 112    | 0     | 23  |
| Coffee    | 1,682  | 0     | 7   |
| Copper    | 62     | 48    | NA  |
| Cotton    | 320    | 256   | 123 |
| Hides     | 70     | NA    | 35  |
| Lead      | 90     | 17    | 10  |
| Meat      | 283    | 37    | 61  |
| Petroleum | 2,457  | 398   | 120 |
| Sugar     | 797    | 29    | 91  |
| Tin       | 57     | 38    | 46  |
| Wheat     | 168    | 438   | 7   |
| Wool      | 181    | 27    | 128 |
| Zinc      | 62     | 18    | 9   |
| Total     | 6,470  | 1,304 | 660 |

Source: International Financial Statistics, February, 1959 (Latin American data), and Vneshniaia Torgovlia SSSR za 1957 god, Moscow, 1958 (Soviet data).

In 1957 about 80% of Latin American exports consisted of the 14 products listed in Table 16. There are four metals—copper, lead, tin, and zinc—and one other mineral—petroleum. Six of the items are food—in each case, quality or luxury foods. There are two fibers, in addition to hides. The Soviet Union produces little and exports no bananas, cacao, or coffee. Thus, for these three products, a potential market can be presumed to exist in the Soviet Union. Consider, however, the nature of these products. Not only does the Soviet Union import very little of them, but also the potential demand for them is among consuming units who have nothing to say about whether or not they will be imported. The effective demand for imports in the Soviet Union is the demand of the planners in the centralized-planning state, and consumer choice, especially in matters of luxury foods, is non-existent. Furthermore, for the most important product, coffee, the Soviet Union has never developed the taste, preferring tea. Eastern Europe also has centralized planning in which the planners' demand for luxury foods is small, but greater than in the Soviet Union. These foods are also discouraged by high excise taxes.

*Soviet Competition.* Among the remaining food products, the Soviet Union is a very substantial net exporter of wheat and thus is a strong competitor of Argentina. Wheat in 1957 was 5% of Soviet exports and was slightly more than twice Argentinian wheat exports of 2,700,000 tons. The Soviet Union's exports more than satisfy Eastern Europe's requirements. The Soviet Union both imports and exports meat and is one of the large meat-producing nations, having made much of its intention to catch up with the United States. Production in 1955 was about 1,300,000 tons, six times its imports that year, and more than 60 times its imports from Argentina in the year of its highest imports from Argentina. The Soviet Union trails Cuba as the second largest sugar producer in the world and its imports of sugar from Cuba in 1957 (the highest year) were 10% of domestic production in 1955. Czechoslovakia is normally an important net sugar exporter.

The Soviet Union imports and exports copper, lead, tin, and zinc. Its net position for the four metals is as a two-for-one net exporter, assuming copper imports are small. In 1956 the Soviet Union, Czechoslovakia, and Poland imported copper, but for the most part Soviet production takes care of its own needs. In 1957 the Soviet Union exported 60,600 tons, more than Mexico exported, about one-half as much as Peru exported, and nearly 15% of Chilean exports of the metal. The Soviet Union exported in 1957 more than twice as much lead and zinc as it imported and is normally at least self-sufficient in these metals. The Soviet Union and Poland export zinc to Western Europe. Tin exports, based on imports from mainland China, have been increasing over the past three years. In most years, the Soviet Union produces enough tin for its own economy. The Soviet Union is a potential competitor when Latin American countries develop their manganese and aluminum industries.

In cotton the Soviet Union exported in 1957 80% as much as Latin America did and has in recent years been a substantial net exporter. Since 1955 there have been growing Soviet "political" imports of cotton from Egypt so that the latter might pay for its arms purchases. While the Soviet Union exports some wool, it is dependent on the outside for some of its requirements. In wool there exists the possibility of a small but significant market in the Soviet Union. Even so, the Soviet Union is seeking to and probably will expand wool production (as well as hides and cotton) and its present marginal dependence will probably become less important.

*Soviet Oil Trade.* The Soviet Union in 1957 exported four times as much crude oil as it imported and nearly three times as much petroleum products. Thus, Venezuela and the Soviet Union are significant competitors. For Argentina, Brazil, and Uruguay, however, Soviet exports of petroleum constitute a raw materials for raw materials complementarity. Latin America, except for Venezuela, is at present in a serious oil deficit position. Oil-cacao, oil-wool, and oil-hides exchanges with these countries constitute, for the short-run, potentially satisfactory transactions. Argentina and Brazil, however, have substantial oil potential and are rapidly exploiting their resources. In less than a decade it is probable that these countries can supply their own needs and perhaps even export.

Significant increases in the living standards of the Soviet Union and Eastern Europe could conceivably result in greater demands for coffee, bananas, cacao, and meat, since imports of these items are a function of the planned rate of change in consumption. It has been a consistent characteristic of Soviet planning, however, that consumption will increase very modestly and even then in such a way that the planners can maintain control over the items of consumption. Large amounts of purchasing power in excess of that which is necessary to maintain a minimum comfort standard of living would give the Soviet consumers the power to influence economic decision-making, by shifting their purchases from one item to another or through savings. Obviously this is not consistent with orderly planning according to Soviet leaders. Furthermore, there are many high priority consumption categories whose present disreputable state will take decades to repair. Housing, for example, is capable of absorbing vast resources before even a minimum comfort standard can be reached. It is highly unlikely, therefore, that rising standards of living in the Soviet Union can be counted upon to open up new markets for Latin America. The situation in Eastern Europe is not quite so dark, but even there large markets for consumption items are improbable.

*Capital Goods Situation.* There is little question as to the great demand for capital goods in Latin America. A significant proportion of its imports consist of machinery and equipment. For example, in 1957 the area as a whole imported about $3.9 billion in capital goods. About $1.0 billion was imported by Venezuela alone. In the machinery and equipment category four countries—Argentina, Brazil, Colombia, and Mexico—imported $1.4 billion in 1957, with Brazil in the lead, having imported $428 million. In previous recent years these amounts have been only slightly less.

The Soviet and East European contribution to this inflow of capital equipment has been minute. Argentina acquired in 1957 $6.6 million of its $305 million in machinery and equipment from the Soviet Union and Eastern Europe, primarily from the latter. Brazil imported only $9.2 million, or less than 2% of its equipment in 1957 from Eastern Europe and none from the Soviet Union. Eastern Europe shipped $2.6 million in machinery and equipment to Uruguay in 1956. It is probable that in 1957 less than $20 million in machinery and equipment was shipped by the Soviet Union and Eastern Europe to all of Latin America, and 95% or more of that amount was provided by Eastern Europe.

While the Soviet Union has been industrializing rapidly and parts of Eastern Europe—notably Czechoslovakia and East Germany—have long been important industrial states, there is a serious question as to their export capability in machinery and equipment. A previous chapter discussed the economic and industrial progress of the Soviet-Eastern European bloc. In trading, the area is a small net exporter of machinery and equipment, based primarily on East German and Czechoslovakian exports. Total machinery and equipment exports of the Soviet Union and Eastern Europe in 1956 and 1957 were less than 40% of Latin American imports of capital goods during those years and the area's total net exports of machinery and equipment were only 18% of Latin America's imports (see Table 17). By itself the Soviet Union is a net importer of machinery and equipment, by $288 million in 1957 and only slightly lesser amounts in 1955 and

Table 17

Soviet Trade in Machinery and Equipment in 1957

(millions of U.S. dollars)

|  | Exports | Imports | Balance |
|---|---|---|---|
| Eastern Europe and China | 535.2 | 720.5 | -185.3 |
| Czechoslovakia | 46.8 | 122.5 | -75.7 |
| East Germany | 17.9 | 399.6 | -381.7 |
| Poland | 60.0 | 91.4 | -31.4 |
| China | 271.6 | 6.4 | +265.2 |
| Others | 138.9 | 100.6 | +38.3 |
| United Kingdom | -- | 29.3 | -29.3 |
| West Germany | -- | 25.3 | -25.3 |
| Latin America | 0.7 | -- | +0.7 |
| Underdeveloped countries, excluding Latin America | 86.0 | -- | +86.0 |
| Other countries | 29.2 | 164.3 | -135.1 |
| Total | 651.1 | 939.4 | -288.3 |

Source:  Vneshniaia Torgovlia SSSR za 1957 god, Moscow, 1958.

1956.  But even these recent relatively modest deficits in capital goods represent a change from the time before the Second World War when Soviet exports of machinery and equipment were negligible.

When one considers that most of the trade in the Soviet-East European bloc is among the countries of the bloc, it is evident that even less is available for export to the outside (see Table 18).  Of the $1,716 million in East European machinery and equipment exports in 1956, $656 million went to the Soviet Union and of the $715 million in Soviet exports, $209 million were shipped to Eastern Europe. Mainland China also claims a large proportion of both Soviet and East European capital goods exports.  The Soviet Union, for example,

Table 18

Soviet and East European Trade in Machinery and Equipment

(millions of U.S. dollars)

|  | 1954 | 1955 | 1956 |
|---|---|---|---|
| **Total** | | | |
| Imports | --- | 1,703 | 1,736 |
| Exports | -- | 2,432 | 2,432 |
| Balance | --- | 729 | 696 |
| **Bulgaria** | | | |
| Imports | 77 | 79 | 105 |
| Exports | 5 | 7 | 12 |
| Balance | -72 | -72 | -93 |
| **Czechoslovakia** | | | |
| Imports | 112 | 140 | 203 |
| Exports | 387 | 511 | 559 |
| Balance | 275 | 371 | 356 |
| **East Germany** | | | |
| Imports | 52 | 55 | --- |
| Exports | 796 | 772 | 802 |
| Balance | 744 | 717 | 802 |
| **Hungary** | | | |
| Imports | 74 | 61 | 56 |
| Exports | 172 | 179 | 149 |
| Balance | 98 | 118 | 93 |
| **Poland** | | | |
| Imports | 294 | 288 | 339 |
| Exports | 96 | 120 | 154 |
| Balance | -198 | -168 | -185 |
| **Rumania** | | | |
| Imports | -- | --- | 72 |
| Exports | --- | --- | 40 |
| Balance | --- | --- | -32 |
| **Soviet Union** | | | |
| Imports | --- | 1,080 | 961 |
| Exports | --- | 843 | 716 |
| Balance | --- | -237 | -245 |

Source:  Economic Survey of Europe, 1957, Economic Commission for Europe, Geneva, 1958, pp. A-53 - A-58.

shipped only $81 million in capital goods in 1956 and $146 million in 1957 to countries other than those of Eastern Europe and mainland China.

Considering the ambitious plans for industrialization embodied in the new Soviet Seven Year Plan, and the corresponding plans for the countries of Eastern Europe, it is apparent that these countries will require nearly all of the machinery and equipment they can produce to approach their plan goals. The amounts which will be left over for export will continue to be marginal. Indeed, the import requirements for capital goods will likely increase substantially, as evidenced by the Khrushchev and Mikoyan pleas for capital equipment on credit from the United States. Accelerated capital goods imports from both Western and Eastern Europe can also be expected. Thus, the Soviet net capital goods import position will probably increase, and while that of Eastern Europe may diminish, its exports will go primarily to the Soviet Union and China.

*     *     *

It is difficult to make a convincing case that the Soviet Union and Eastern Europe either now or in the future will provide a significant market for Latin American export products. It is equally unconvincing to argue that the Soviet-East European bloc can be a significant supplier of machinery and equipment to Latin America. Quite small amounts of trade are likely, but there is no evidence that the degree of complementarity is sufficient to warrant a substantial scale of trade on an economic basis. Indeed, it is probable that competition will increase, as Latin American oil development proceeds and as the Soviet Union begins to compete even more vigorously in metals.

Given a sufficiently high political priority, larger-scale trade between the Soviet-East European area and Latin America would be possible. Such a review of the Soviet priority schedule would imply an economic cost to the Soviet Union, a lower priority for other areas, and hence the risk of political loss there, in anticipation of political gain in Latin America. Political trade of this nature does not seem likely on any significant scale for Latin America, although it is always possible. Latin America's basic geographic, economic, and political position does not appear to be subject to significant change by any actions which are realistically within Soviet capabilities.

What, finally, can be said about trade and economic relations between Latin American countries and the Soviet Union and Eastern Europe? Will trade grow and become of great significance? Will it always be small but still provide an entering wedge for influencing vital political decisions? Perhaps the best way to evaluate these economic relations and their implications and to answer these questions is to seek the answers to another series of questions:

1. What trends exist in Latin American trade and economic relations with the Soviet Union and Eastern Europe?

2. Will Soviet and East European trade performance improve?

3. What policies will guide these economic relations?

4. Will Soviet and East European credit play an important role in their economic relations with Latin America?

5. What are the prospects for trade between the two areas?

6. Will Soviet and East European influence in Latin America increase?

*Trends.* One of the most notable characteristics of economic relations between these two huge continental areas is that trade is not only small in magnitude but also displays no significant trend in volume. The highest level of trade was in 1955. Following a decline in 1956, volume has increased in 1957 and 1958, as it did in the years preceding 1955. The general level of trade is higher in the late 1950's but has been quite unstable from year to year. Single transactions in the low and erratic volume of trade loom so large that an incipient trend can readily be reversed in any given year. There is no evidence of departure from the high degree of concentration of the trade in a few Latin American countries—Argentina, Brazil, and Uruguay—or the predominance of Eastern Europe, especially Czechoslovakia and Poland.

*Trade Performance.* The performance of the Soviet Union and Eastern Europe has been sufficiently unsatisfactory and the Latin American response sufficiently vocal that an improvement can be expected. Some elements are under the control of the Soviet-East European traders, such as availability of items, deliveries, and quality.

Other elements, particularly the pricing system, which automatically worsens Latin American terms of trade, are inherent in centralized planning and state trading. The only remedy is a conscious effort on the part of the Soviet Union and Eastern Europe to favor Latin America with price concessions. It is possible that this course may be followed from time to time. More than likely, however, state trading organizations will continue to behave much as they do at the present time, but with a more concerted effort to avoid offending Latin American countries.

*Policies.* The framework of bilateralism with formal trade agreements will undoubtedly continue. Because of the pressure of Latin America, however, the bilateral balancing aspects will probably weaken and the use of convertible and transferable currencies increase. The agreements themselves will probably be increasingly liberalized, abandoning the unrealistic quotas and even total trade targets. It is possible that the number of agreements, although permissive in character, may increase at the insistence of the Soviet Union and Eastern Europe, primarily because state trading organs feel they can do business only with an agreement. The Soviet-East European efforts to increase trade through fairs, exhibits, advertising, and other trade promotion devices, will no doubt persist.

*Credit.* For the most part so far Latin America has made short-term, current account loans to the Soviet Union and Eastern Europe, rather than the other way around. Argentina has been offered several specific loans, the latest being the $100 million oil development loan, but only insignificant amounts have been delivered to that or any other country in Latin America. It is possible that more offers will be made and there may be some deliveries. Given, however, the absence of any demonstrated or potential capability of the Soviet Union to export capital goods, which is the basis of most intermediate or long-term credit, in any large volume, it is quite unlikely that Latin America can acquire any sizeable amounts of capital equipment with delayed payments.

*Prospects.* Credit is, of course, only one aspect of trade. The prospects for any greatly enlarged trade, at least based on economic considerations, are slim. The structure of the Latin American economies is such that they are not able to supply to the Soviet Union and Eastern Europe the kinds of products which that area has any really effective demand for, and the Soviet Union and Eastern Europe are not prepared to provide Latin America with any significant proportion of the latter's needs for capital goods. It is possible that trade could grow by as much as 50% in the next decade, but such an expansion would not necessarily represent an increase in the proportion of total trade for the Soviet-East European area. The higher degree of complementarity with Eastern Europe implies that trade with that area may experience relatively greater growth than with the Soviet Union. It should be recognized that if the Soviet Union and Eastern Europe decide on such a course, trade could be expanded substantially because of political considerations. In this event, the Soviet-East European area would simply create an artificial complementarity and absorb whatever costs were involved. Such trade would likely be quite unstable and unless the present unfavorable Latin American economic conditions continue unabated or even become worse, it is likely that Latin American countries would tend to be conservative about "political" trade.

*Influence.* It seems almost certain that Soviet and East European influence in Latin America will increase, but it is equally certain that Latin American countries will continuously be on their guard against any external influence which will affect vital decisions. Trade and economic relations have had relatively little influence on Latin America so far and much of that has been in the direction of greater caution and suspicion of the Soviet Union and Eastern Europe. The favorable impact has come rather from the continued economic successes of the Soviet Union, its economic growth, and its attainment of respectability as a nation. The fear of Communism and the Soviet Union indicated by some Western countries assists in the growth of Soviet influence in areas such as Latin America, since the latter sees the conflict as an opportunity to play one power off against the other. There is little doubt, however, that Latin American countries are fully conscious that their self-interest is inextricably bound to the West and will probably be able to ward off successfully any attempt at external economic and political domination.

\*   \*   \*

The experiences of Latin America in trade with the Soviet Union and Eastern Europe point to some larger lessons for other countries. First and foremost, the enthusiasm of new-found trading relations must be tempered by a soul-searching examination of the fundamental economic basis for trade. For Latin America, and for some other areas such as the Middle East, large-scale trading relations with the Soviet Union and Eastern Europe are precluded, on economic grounds at least, on the basis of inadequate complementarity and on large-scale competition. Latin American trade also points to pitfalls in the operation of trade with the Soviet-East European area, on three levels: Bilateral trade and payments agreements, the use of non-convertible currencies, and state trading. These inhibit the growth of trade and make mutually beneficial trade the exception rather than the rule. These devices also imply an automatic deterioration in the terms of trade of the primary producing country trying to do business with the Soviet Union and Eastern Europe. Latin American trade with the Soviet-East European area is not an isolated example. It is a part of the complex pattern of political, ideological, and economic interests which the Soviet Union seeks to promote in all of its activities in all areas, with the ultimate goal of world domination.

# REFERENCES

## Chapter I

1. Eastern Europe consists of Bulgaria, Czechoslovakia, East Germany, Hungary, Poland, and Rumania. Albania and mainland China are excluded on the basis of the principle of *de minimis*. Latin America as used in this paper means the twenty republics.

## Chapter II

1. There are several sets of basic data on Latin American trade with the Soviet Union and Eastern Europe. The fundamental sources are the national statistical reports of the trading partners. International organizations, particularly the United Nations and its Economic Commission for Latin America and the International Monetary Fund collect these data and report them in dollars in such publications as *Direction of International Trade,* and *Economic Survey (s) of Latin America.* The United States Department of Commerce, Bureau of Foreign Commerce, International Economic Analysis Division, also reports collected data in its *Value Series* and *Country by Commodity Series.*
2. Robert Loring Allen, "A Note on Soviet Foreign Trade Statistics," *Soviet Studies,* April, 1959.

## Chapter III

1. The Soviet Union and Eastern Europe have definitely exercised the initiative in promoting bilateral agreements. A. E. Manenok and V. V. Rogov, Soviet writers, explained the wide year-to-year variations in trade thus: "One of the real reasons for the fluctuation in Soviet-Argentinian trade was the lack of the necessary agreement on the basic laws of trade. The Soviet government, wishing to create such a basis, suggested to the Argentinian government that it sign a trade agreement on the same basis that the Soviet government was signing with other countries." See V. P. Gorunov, N. N. Inozemstsev, and V. B. Spandarian (editors), *Vneshniaia Torgovlia SSSR so stranami Asii, Afriki, i Latinskoi Ameriki,* Moscow, 1958, p. 181. Later, in the same book, they say: "The signing of the trade agreement between the USSR and Argentina created a realistic basis for the development of trade between the two countries." *Ibid.,* p. 184.
2. Data on trade and payments agreements and other accords can be found in *International Trade News Bulletin,* General Agreement on Tariffs and Trade, Geneva, 1951-1958; *Exchange Restrictions,* First to Ninth Annual Reports, International Monetary Fund, Washington, 1950-1958; *Trade Agreements and Other Trade Accords with Soviet Bloc Countries,* U.S. Department of State, Washington, 1955-1958; *The Soviet Bloc Role in Free World Economic Enterprises and Development Projects,* Report of the Economic Defense Advisory Committee, International Cooperation Administration, Washington, 1956; *Foreign Assistance Activities of the Communist Bloc and Their Implication for the United States,* A Study by the Council for Economic and Industry Research, for the

**105**

Special Senate Committee to Study the Foreign Aid Program, Washington, 1957; and such North American newspapers as the *New York Times, Christian Science Monitor,* and *Wall Street Journal.* A comprehensive tabulation of all Soviet and East European agreements can be found in Raymond Mikesell and Jack Behrman, *Financing Free World Trade with the Sino-Soviet Bloc,* International Finance Section, Princeton, 1958, Appendix I.

3. *International Affairs* (Moscow), October, 1958, quoted in *Soviet News,* Press Department of the Soviet Embassy in London, No. 3940, October, 1958, p. 76.

## CHAPTER IV

1. Soviet organs use the United States as one of their favorite whipping boys in this respect. For example, see M. Zakhmatov, "The Export of Private Capital from the USA as a Means of Capturing Foreign Markets," *Vneshniaia Torgovlia,* No. 7, 1958, pp. 8-14. In particular, Brazil is accused of being under foreign influence in its trade in I. Bunegina, "Certain Problems of Brazil's Economy and Foreign Trade," *ibid.,* pp. 14-20.

2. Noting that "the government of Argentina wants to refuse trade contracts formed on the basis of bilateral governmental agreements and strives to replace them by a system of multilateral trade based on payments in convertible currencies," A. I. Manenok and V. V. Rogov assert that "the foreign trade policy of the new government and the changes instituted in the system of regulating foreign trade serve only the interests of those Argentinian circles which are closely tied with American and English markets." See *Vneshniaia Torgovlia SSSR so stranami Asii, Afriki, i Latinskoi Ameriki,* cited, p. 187.

3. Joseph Stalin, *Economic Problems of Socialism in the U.S.S.R.,* International Publishers, New York, 1952, p. 26. This highly touted new doctrine is presumably intended to elevate to the status of equality the "socialist" with the "capitalist" market. In fact it displays an amazing credulity about international markets, the operation of foreign trade, and the elementary principles of production and exchange.

4. *Vneshniaia Torgovlia SSSR za 1957 god,* Moscow, 1958, pp. 17, 127.

## CHAPTER V

1. Statistical data for this section are taken primarily from the *World Economic Survey* (s), *Economic Survey* (s) of *Latin America, Economic Bulletin* (s) *for Latin America, Statistical Yearbook* (s), all published by the United Nations, New York; *Direction of International Trade,* Joint Publication of the Statistical Office of the United Nations, International Monetary Fund, and International Bank for Reconstruction and Development; and *International Financial Statistics,* International Monetary Fund, Washington.

## CHAPTER VI

1. Latin America shares the motives and goals of many primary producing countries. For a general characterization of these objectives, see Mikesell and Behrman, *op. cit.,* especially Chapter II, and for particular countries see Robert Loring Allen,

"Burma's Clearing Account Agreements," *Pacific Affairs*, June, 1958, pp. 147-163, and "The Vulnerability of Iceland's Economy," *Finanz-Archiv*, April, 1959.

2.  *New Times* (Moscow), No. 46, November, 1958, pp. 18-19.

3.  *New York Times*, October 2, 1958.

4.  *New York Times*, April 1, 1956; June 17, 18, 19, 20, 1956; July 21, 22, 1956; October 24, 1958.

5.  Robert J. Alexander, *Communism in Latin America*, Rutgers University Press, New Brunswick, New Jersey, 1957, is an authoritative and detailed descriptive analysis of the Communist movement in Latin America.

6.  U Raschid, Burma's trade minister, said something very close to this: "We have rice to sell and we must sell it if we are to survive. If we cannot sell it for cash, we will sell it under clearing account arrangements." *Burma Commerce*, February 19, 1956.

CHAPTER VII

1.  Two recent studies are valuable: Jan Wszelaki, *Communist Economic Strategy: The Role of East Central Europe*, National Planning Association, Washington, 1959, and Alec Nove, *Communist Economic Strategy: Soviet Capabilities and Growth*, National Planning Association, Washington, forthcoming. See also Harry Schwartz, *Russia's Soviet Economy*. Prentice-Hall, Englewood Cliffs, New Jersey, second edition, 1954; Nicholas Spulber, *The Economics of Communist Eastern Europe*, Technology Press and John Wiley & Sons, New York, 1957; *Trends in Economic Growth, A Comparison of the Western Powers and the Soviet Bloc*, Legislative Reference Service, Library of Congress for the Joint Committee on the Economic Report, Government Printing Office, Washington, 1955.

2.  Testimony of Douglas Dillon to the Senate Foreign Relations Committee, March 3, 1958, in *Review of Foreign Policy, 1958*, Part I, Government Printing Office, Washington, 1958, p. 303, gives the figure as $170 billion. There are many technical difficulties in computing Soviet product in U.S. dollars. It perhaps would be more appropriate to use a range of $130 billion to $170 billion to cover the numerous estimates by reputable scholars.

3.  The Chairman of the Brazilian Delegation to the Special Committee of the 21 Latin American Republics, Mr. Augusto F. Schmidt, presented a paper giving Soviet growth at 10% per year from now until 1980. This figure is higher than even the Soviet Union claims for its industrial growth, and does not recognize, as even the Soviet Union does, that the rate of growth is declining, and indicates only that Soviet claims have made a very erroneous impression in Latin America. Later Mr. Schmidt, a lyric poet, denied that the figures were a prediction, stating that the "estimate would be conditioned upon the continuance of various factors which now affect these economies." (*Washington Post*, December 18, 1958). If by this he means that if Soviet growth continues to be 10%, it will continue to be 10%, he is certainly right. Continuance of the various factors cannot, by definition in the context of growth, exist.

CHAPTER VIII

1.  This aspect of trade has been closely examined in Joseph Berliner, *Soviet Economic Aid*, Frederick A. Praeger, New York, 1958, particularly Chapter VII; Mikesell

and Behrman, *op. cit.*, particularly Chapter II; Robert Loring Allen, "Economic Motives in Soviet Foreign Trade Policy," *Southern Economic Journal,* October, 1958, pp. 189-201; Stanley J. Zyzniewski, "The Soviet Bloc and Under-developed Countries: Some Economic Factors," *World Politics,* April, 1959.

2. The visit of Anastas Mikoyan to the United States in January, 1959, is evidence of continued Soviet equipment needs. His bargaining position was weakened, however, by the Soviet desire to import principally items on the strategic trade control list, as well as his demand for long-term government credit in the face of a large outstanding debt to the United States.

3. Chapter IX examines the competitive and complementary aspects of trade in detail.

4. V. B. Spandarian in *Vneshniaia Torgovlia SSSR so stranami Asii, Afriki, i Latinskoi Ameriki,* cited, pp. 5-6, gives the official motives as "The Soviet Union in its foreign policy is guided by the principle of offering support to the countries seeking national and economic independence from the colonial powers. On that basic principle the Soviet Union is also building its economic relations with the countries of Asia, Africa, and Latin America, which are seeking independent development of their own." The Soviet Union tends to regard economic development as industrialization through centralized planning and independence as a neutralist or pro-Soviet posture.

5. For a detailed discussion of these trends including a statistical analysis, see Robert Loring Allen, "Economic Motives in Soviet Foreign Trade Policy," cited, pp. 189-201.

6. See Berliner, *op. cit.*, pp. 119-136.

7. Wszelaki, *op. cit.*, pp. 5-32.

8. "Soviet Diplomatic Relations," *Intelligence Information Brief,* No. 51, Department of State, Washington, December, 1958, and other data supplied by the State Department.

9. *International Affairs* (Moscow), December, 1957, and *O Cruziero,* October, 1958, as reported in *Soviet News,* Press Department of the Soviet Embassy, London, No. 3739, December 6, 1957, pp. 165-166; No. 3940, October 30, 1958, p. 76; and *New York Times,* March 2, 1958; October 21, 1958.

10. "World Strength of the Communist Party Organizations," *Intelligence Report,* No. 4489, Department of State, Washington, January, 1959, pp. 82-95.